RECEIVED
2 3 OCT 2006

Moreton Morrell Site

DK business *masters*

658·0092

KT-144-761

andrew
GROVE

ROBERT HELLER

WITHDRAWN
WARWICKSHIRE
COLLEGE
LIBRARY

Warwickshire College

00529761

Dorling Kindersley

LONDON, NEW YORK, SYDNEY, DELHI, PARIS,
MUNICH & JOHANNESBURG

Managing Editor Adèle Hayward
Senior Art Editor Jamie Hanson
DTP Designer Julian Dams
Production Controller Michelle Thomas

Senior Managing Editor Stephanie Jackson
Senior Managing Art Editor Nigel Duffield

Produced for Dorling Kindersley by
Grant Laing Partnership
48 Brockwell Park Gardens,
London SE24 9BJ
Managing Editor Jane Laing
Project Editor Helen Ridge
Managing Art Editor Steve Wilson

First published in Great Britain in 2001
by Dorling Kindersley Limited,
9 Henrietta Street, London WC2E 8PS

2 4 6 8 10 9 7 5 3 1

Copyright © 2001
Dorling Kindersley Limited, London
Text copyright © 2001 Robert Heller

The right of Robert Heller to be identified
as the author of this book has been asserted
in accordance with the Copyright, Designs,
and Patents Act 1988, Sections 77 and 78.

All rights reserved. No part of this
publication may be reproduced, stored in a
retrieval system, or transmitted in any
form or by any means, electronic,
mechanical, photocopying, recording, or
otherwise, without the prior written
permission of the copyright owner.

A CIP catalogue record for this book is
available from the British Library

ISBN 0 7513 1275 4

Reproduced by Colourpath, London
Printed in Hong Kong by Wing King Tong

see our complete catalogue at
www.dk.com

Author's Acknowledgments
The many sources for this book have been
acknowledged in the text, but I must now
express my great debt to everybody, above
all to the Mastermind himself. Nor would
the book exist but for the inspiration and
effort of the excellent Dorling Kindersley
team – to whom my warm thanks.

Packager's Acknowledgments
Grant Laing Partnership would like to
thank the following for their help and
participation:
Index Kay Ollerenshaw
Picture Research Anna Grapes

Picture Credits
The publisher would like to thank the
following for their kind permission to
reproduce the following photographs:
Associated Press AP: David Breslauer 56;
Camera Press: Stuart Mark 26; **Corbis UK
Ltd:** Underwood and Underwood 35, Galen
Rowell 70, Roger Ressmeyer 97; **Katz
Pictures:** Nigel Parry/Cpi 1, 4, William
Mercer Mcleod/Outline 9; **Science &
Society Picture Library:** 47, 63, 87;
Science Photo Library: Erich Schrempp
88; **Frank Spooner Pictures:** Peter
Smith/Liaison 75; **Tony Stone Images:**
Andy Sacks 12, Joe McBride 48.

Contents

Warwickshire College
Library
Moreton Morrell Centre

Class No:

Acc No:

Strategic guru
and driving force

Andrew S. Grove and Bill Gates are the prime managerial architects of the digital revolution. Although Gates has by far the higher visibility, partly because of his enormous wealth, it is Grove who deserves the loftier ranking. Grove is no more a technological genius than Gates, but as business manager he led the unmatched wave of superb innovations – above all, the microprocessor – that created Intel's success, achieving sales that are much greater than Microsoft's. Where Gates advanced by matching the innovations of others, such as the graphical user interface or the browser, Intel has been the driving force in breaking new technological ground, with Grove as the driving force behind Intel.

He has written an invaluable record of how Intel was driven, and has given clear, stimulating advice to would-be leaders who want to follow suit. Paying the same passionate attention to detail as to critical strategic change, Grove has bridged every mega-trend, from the PC to the Internet, which Intel was confronting as he stepped up to be chairman in 1997. He has no superior in management either as strategic exponent or strategic guru.

Robert Heller

Andrew S. Grove, known far and wide as "Andy", was born András Gróf in Hungary in 1936. When the Germans moved into Hungary during the Second World War, his Jewish family went into hiding and emerged only after the German defeat. Hungary remained inhospitable, though, under Soviet domination, which culminated in the savage repression of the 1956 uprising. Then a student, Grove had been active in the failed revolution, and he wisely fled to the United States.

An uncle living in New York took Grove in. He started studying chemical engineering at City College, and what followed was a typical story of self-help and achievement, American-style. Working his way through college as a waiter, he came top of his class. The honours degree opened the door to the University of Southern California at Berkeley, where Grove took his PhD in 1963. He was by then married to Eva, a fellow Hungarian; they have two daughters.

Unusually, Grove has combined business and academic careers. While serving as one of America's most famous CEOs at Intel, he taught a class in strategic management at Stanford University's business school. Much earlier, as a young researcher at Fairchild Camera, he lectured at Berkeley. He had chosen his main employer well, though: Fairchild became, and rightly so, a legendary name in the history of microelectronics.

The roots of Fairchild Camera went back to the famous development of the transistor at Bell Laboratories in 1948 under William Shockley. After helping Schockley start his own lab, eight team members deserted him to launch their own venture. Nicknamed "The Traitorous Eight", they were given $1.5 million of finance by the playboy entrepreneur Sherman Fairchild, and started making semiconductors. The new business prospered, but, in 1967, after a decade of increasing fame and internal troubles, the "Traitors" started to go their separate ways, and, in 1968, two of the brightest and best, Robert Noyce and Gordon Moore, left the organization.

Grove's brilliant career is inseparable from the epochal achievements of these two men. Noyce is the father of the "integrated circuit" – the piece of silicon containing many transistors, which is at the heart of the electronic devices that have changed the world. He was general manager at Fairchild, and Moore head of R&D. Another engineering genius, Moore became famous for "Moore's Law": that the performance of integrated circuitry would double every 18 months at constant prices; that is, the price of a given amount of power would halve. In hiring the 32-year-old Andy Grove, the pair formed the triumvirate whose breakaway, named Intel, became the King of Silicon Valley.

At that time, Grove sported gold chain and mutton-chop whiskers, as well as frizzy brown hair and a Hungarian accent. The later, more conservative Grove has lost most of the accent, but still favours the Valley's shirt-sleeved, tieless style. He is physically energetic, with the lean look of a keen mountain-biker. Meticulous and a stickler for punctuality, enormously hard-working, and something of a control freak, Grove is clever, highly organized, and confident.

In 1968, however, he was not a manufacturing expert, and was hardly qualified to be Intel's "Director of Operations". But this was a man who would thrust himself and his company forward. In theory, Bob Graham, also from Fairchild, might have seized the number three position, but, by the time of Graham's delayed arrival to head marketing, Grove had hired "dozens of engineers and managers... and to him... they established their first loyalty", as Tim Jackson notes in his book *Inside Intel* (1997).

"Grove took on more responsibility than he otherwise might have done. Who does what is always vague in a start-up; an intelligent, energetic person with a eye for detail who is willing to do the things that others have left behind can become considerably more powerful than his job role would suggest. And Andy Grove was the ultimate details guy."

The best manager in the world

The biography of Andy Grove from 1968 is the story of Intel and of how he developed into "the best manager in the world", according to *Fortune* magazine. By 1974 – the crucial year when Intel launched the 8008 microprocessor – Grove was executive vice-president and official Third Man. Noyce had become chairman and, as the company's front man, he was now less involved in the strategic and technological decisions; Moore dominated these as CEO. Everything else came under Grove.

In 1979, Grove was promoted to president, and, in 1987, became chief executive. By then Noyce and Moore were pushing 60. They had masterminded an astonishing run of technological breakthroughs: the first memory chip, the first DRAM ("dynamic random access memory"), the first EPROM ("erasable, programmable, read-only memory"), and the first microprocessor. Just as important, all four innovations had been exploited commercially to lucrative effect; for this Grove deserves much of the credit.

As the devices poured out of his fabrication plants ("fabs", as they are known), so Intel's sales and profits soared. It was not, however, a story of smooth progress; nor did it happen without strenuous effort or crisis. When it comes to effort or critical threats, though, Grove is in his element.

Goading, challenging, bullying, shouting, he never relaxes the pressure for results or for relevance: in his office, a neat 2.5-m by 2.7-m (8-ft by 9-ft) cubicle surrounded by similar cubicles, there is a hand-held wooden sign for use at meetings: IS THERE A QUESTION HERE OR IS IT A SPEECH?

Grove's driving, ambitious, take-no-prisoners personality is ideal for the highly combative climate of Silicon Valley. To all intents and purposes, Intel under Grove won a near-monopoly of microprocessors that was (and is) every bit as strong as that of Microsoft in operating software. But

Combining drive and vision
Grove applied his enormous energy and strategic thinking to steering Intel through the key crisis points in its history, as it capitalized on key advances in digital technology.

while just as committed as Bill Gates to preserving his supremacy, and just as fierce in protecting it, Grove has navigated the rapids more adroitly.

Intel's dealings with rivals have been combative in the extreme. Negotiations with the anti-trust authorities resulted in a 1998 consent decree that restrained Intel's competitive conduct, but which saved it from the legal embarrassments in which Microsoft became entangled. The company's unremitting enactment of Moore's Law, moreover, satisfied the PC makers with a continuous, dramatic improvement in microprocessor power, availability, and price/performance ratio, which, in turn, spurred the PC market again and again.

A practical intellectual

Throughout this rumbustious career, Grove not only retained his academic connections, but also wrote newspaper columns and books. His first book, *Physics and Technology of Semiconductor Devices* (1967), was a clear account, full of mathematics. *High Output Management*, published in 1983, broke new, non-technical ground. This is not a book about the achievements and thoughts of a self-publicizing tycoon. It is a textbook on how to maximize managerial effectiveness. The first chapter explains "The Basics of Production" by discussing and analyzing the service of breakfast in a hotel (one of Grove's first jobs). How do you get a three-minute egg, buttered toast, and coffee to the customer simultaneously and piping hot? The answer was an analogy for developing "a clear understanding of the trade-offs between the various factors – manpower, capacity, and inventory" and how you "must reduce the understanding to a quantifiable set of relationships".

That passage gives an excellent picture of the special qualities of Grove's mind. He is the practical intellectual *par excellence*, as he demonstrated again with his 1996 book *Only the Paranoid Survive*, whose catchy title expresses a powerful idea: that, without unremitting vigilance and strenuous action, success will corrode into failure. That fear only reflects the realities of Intel's industry, and of the many major and minor threats that Grove has overcome.

In every difficult situation, Grove has combined necessary toughness with rare adaptability. His book, typically for Grove, turns insight into incisive, fact-based theory. The combination has helped to create vast wealth for Intel's investors. Grove has naturally shared in those proceeds: in a single year — 1996 — Grove pocketed nearly $95 million in stock options. The next year Grove became chairman as well as CEO, and in 1998 he relinquished his CEO title to Craig Barrett. This was doubly understandable: Grove was 62 and had suffered from prostate cancer.

The illness provided another demonstration of Grove's formidable personality. He thoroughly researched all the latest information available on the cancer before deciding on the appropriate treatment. Then he published a full and frank account of the entire experience in *Fortune*. To achieve such a degree of detachment when threatened with death shows enormous courage and much scientific curiosity.

These qualities were both essential in Grove's lifework. He was not the author of Intel's technological miracles, but he made them happen by taking and controlling the colossal risks and sums involved; one of his beloved "fabs" can cost as much as $2 billion. The methods and management philosophy that he describes so honestly and succinctly will leave generations of managers, as well as Intel investors, heavily in his debt.

1

Raising management output

Using delegation to achieve high managerial leverage ● The three basics of business management ● **Where the art of management comes in** ● How to turn your calendar into a productivity tool ● **Making meetings more effective as the key medium of managerial work** ● The four conditions that must be met before a meeting is justified ● **The three-stage process – free discussion, clarity, and full commitment – for good decision-making** ● Overcoming the "peer-group syndrome"

Andy Grove published *High Output Management* in 1983, when two decades of unprecedented turbulence lay ahead of both his company and management in general. Two developments in particular had profound impact on Intel: the upsurge of Japanese competition and the digital revolution, which gathered momentum as the applications of the new technology conquered the world. The first drove Intel out of the memory industry, which it had founded; the second confronted the company with new opportunities and threats.

Yet, despite the upheavals, Grove found that, in the mid-1990s, "most of the things that were useful [in 1983] are still useful now; the basics of management remain largely unaffected". That applies to the three ideas on which Grove's book was founded:

■ The principles and discipline of manufacturing apply to other forms of business enterprise, including most emphatically the work of managers.
■ The output of managers is the output of the organizational units under their supervision or influence.
■ A team will perform well only if peak performance is obtained from its individual members.

All three ideas are naturally based on Grove's experiences at Intel. They may read like statements of the obvious, even the second, which Grove italicizes as "the single most important sentence of this book". But good management does largely consist of the practice of the obvious. The force of Grove's ideas lies in their clarity and in the practical rigour with which he developed them, both in running Intel and in developing his "output-oriented approach to management" into a coherent, cogent theory.

Obvious or not, Grove's definition of management output is not shared by most executives. When he asked a group of middle managers at Intel what they understood by the term, they described activity, not output, which is "by no means the same thing". Their replies were:

- judgements and opinions
- direction
- allocation of resources
- mistakes detected
- personnel trained, subordinates developed
- courses taught
- products planned
- commitments negotiated

None of them talked about teamwork, although to Grove this is fundamental: "Business... is a team activity. And, always, it takes a team to win." Here Grove is discussing people contributing to a common output, not people working together in groups. As a CEO, he affected output by supervising his direct subordinates. He also influenced groups not under his direct supervision "by making observations and suggestions to those who manage them".

What managers do

Grove analysed a day of his own in order "to find out what we managers really do". In a long day (over 12 hours), he spent an hour at lunch with Intel associates, three-and-a-quarter hours either alone or with one other person, six hours in meetings, and two hours giving an "orientation" lecture to professional employees (giving and gathering information, and acting as role model). The desk-time was devoted to garnering information, decision-making, and "nudging" – Grove's gentle word for pushing people strongly in a certain direction.

The meetings, including lunch, were spent mostly on gathering information, with some decision-making and nudging, not necessarily by Grove. He admits that the day shows no obvious pattern, but concludes that much of his day passed in acquiring information in every way possible:

> "I read standard reports and memos but also get information ad hoc. I talk to people inside and outside the company, managers at other firms or financial analysts, or members of the press. Customer complaints, both internal and external, are also a very important source of information."

Grove's guiding principle, though, is to shift his energy and attention to whatever will most increase the output of the organization. In his words, managers should move to the point where their "leverage will be the greatest".

Getting high leverage

Leverage is a central concept for Grove. He works by an equation that says that for every activity performed by a manager, the output of the organization should increase to some extent. The greater the increase, the higher the leverage. This has a direct link with productivity (output in a given unit of time), which can be raised by:

- increasing the speed at which a manager performs
- increasing the leverage associated with the various managerial activities
- shifting the mix of a manager's activities from those with lower leverage to those with higher leverage

Grove lists three basic ways in which high leverage can be achieved: first, when many people are affected by one manager; second, when somebody else's work or behaviour over a long period of time is affected by a manager's brief and well-focused set of words or actions; third, when the work of a large group is affected by an individual who supplies a unique, key piece of knowledge or information.

The leverage concept is used to reinforce familiar instructions to managers: for instance, that they should prepare in advance of planning; act in a timely fashion; create a "tickler" file (to trigger enquiries into progress); and arrive fully prepared for meetings. "A manager can also exert high leverage by... an activity that takes... only a short time, but that affects another person's performance over a long time." An example here is a properly prepared performance review.

Examples of high negative leverage are numerous, including depressed, waffling, and meddling managers. With his scientific language ("leverage") and his equation, Grove seems to be constructing a scientific approach to management. But he also recognizes an "art of management", which "lies in the capacity to select from the many activities of seemingly comparable significance the one or two or three that provide leverage well beyond the others" and to concentrate on these. Paying close attention to customer complaints is one such high leverage activity:

"Which one out of 10 or 20 complaints to dig into, analyze, and follow up is where art comes into the work of a manager. The basis of that art is an intuition that behind this complaint and not the other lurk many deeper problems."

Delegation has high leverage when it is effective, low when the delegator clings to the work. Grove insists that "delegator" and "delegate" must share "a common information base and a common set of operational ideas or notions on how to go about solving problems". He adds that this requirement is frequently not met, and that often emotion comes into play: "We all have some things that we don't really *want* to delegate simply because we like doing them and would rather not let go."

Monitoring delegation

Clinging to enjoyable tasks that could be delegated is permissible, in Grove's view, so long as that choice is conscious. He advises you to delegate familiar tasks before the unfamiliar. Doing so facilitates the essential task of monitoring to ensure that delegation is going according to plan. He draws an analogy between monitoring delegation and the principles of quality assurance:

- Monitor at the stage where least value has been added (thus, review rough drafts of requested reports, instead of waiting for the final version).
- Vary the frequency. Increase or decrease the incidence of monitoring based on delegate's experience with a specific task and their previous performance.
- Go into details only at random.
- Monitor delegated decisions by concentrating on the process the delegate has used in thinking them through.

Delegation is one way of increasing a manager's output per hour. Other methods include time-management, which Grove treats in a perfunctory way, partly because he thinks his production principles are superior. First, he seeks the "limiting step", the element around which others have to revolve. In his own case, teaching duties have this role, because he must meet the class at the given time: "if we determine what is immovable and manipulate the more yielding activities around it, we can work more efficiently".

You can also "batch" similar tasks to save on "set-up time". If you have several reports to read, set aside a block of time and do a batch together. Another applicable production technique is forecasting, which is useful for much managerial work. The medium of a manager's forecast is the calendar, which most people use as repository of "orders" received. Grove calls this "mindless passivity". His calendar is a productivity tool:

■ Use your calendar actively. Use your initiative to fill the holes between time-critical events with necessary activities that are not time-critical.

■ Say "no" at the outset to any work beyond your capacity.

Grove advises that you should say "no" earlier rather than later. Remember, too, that time is your only finite resource: "when you say 'yes' to one thing you are inevitably saying 'no' to another". Moreover, your ability to say "no" will be needed in applying another production principle: "slack", or "a bit of looseness in your scheduling". Do not load your schedule beyond the optimum degree; then "one unanticipated phone call will not ruin your schedule for the rest of the day". Another of Grove's production principles is very nearly the opposite of allowing slack:

"What is 'nice' or 'not nice' should have no place in how you think or what you do. Remember, we are after what is most effective." *High Output Management*

"A manager should carry a raw material *inventory* in terms of projects... this inventory should consist of things you need to do but don't need to finish right away.... Without such an inventory of projects, a manager will most probably use his free time meddling in his subordinates' work."

If there are too many or too few subordinates, leverage is reduced, so Grove recommends six to eight for a supervisory manager, and suggests that half a day per week be allocated to each person. A similar calculation covers the "know-how manager", who supplies mainly expertise and information. Grove reckons that half a day spent in a planning, advisory, or co-ordinating group is equivalent to having one subordinate. If your job combines supervision and know-how, the number of subordinates should be reduced accordingly.

Handling interruptions

The more subordinates you have, the more interruptions you will experience. An experiment at Intel revealed that the output of supervisors and know-how managers was limited primarily by uncontrolled interruptions. Grove can only offer tips to deal with the problem: do not hide away; develop standard responses for standard interruptions; schedule an open hour when anybody can come in; batch interruptions and handle the issues at staff meetings and "one-on-ones".

Grove calls meetings "the medium of managerial work", where managers supply information and know-how, guide the groups under their control and influence, and make and help to make decisions. He says that these tasks can "only occur during face-to-face encounters and therefore only during meetings" – a generalization that is self-evidently untrue, but which reflects the specific culture at Intel.

Intel has three kinds of "process-oriented meetings", where knowledge is shared and exchanged. Grove is famous for his "one-on-ones" with subordinates, which are regularly scheduled, a practice that he believes "highly unusual outside of Intel". The habit sprang from his early days with the company, when he knew little about either memory chips or manufacturing techniques and therefore scheduled regular tutorials with two subordinates who could cure his ignorance. One-on-ones, lasting at least an hour, remain Grove's chief recommendation for learning, finding things out, and managing individuals.

Staff meetings

Grove believes that staff meetings are also "key to good management", because they allow peer interaction, including decision-making; the supervisor can also learn from the exchange of views. Grove develops a much better understanding of an issue by listening to two people with opposing views than by hearing one side only. He prefers these meetings to work to an agenda but also includes an "open session". He asks a key question:

"What is the role of the supervisor in the staff meeting – a leader, observer, expediter, questioner, decision-maker? The answer, of course, is all of them... A supervisor should never use staff meetings to pontificate, which is the surest way to undermine free discussion and hence the meeting's basic purpose."

Grove's third category of meetings – operation reviews – is "the medium of interaction for people who don't otherwise have much opportunity to deal with one another". The format here should include formal presentations in which managers describe their work to other managers who are not their immediate supervisors, and to peers in other parts of the company. These are teaching and learning occasions, in which each of the players has a distinct role: the organizing manager, the reviewing manager, the presenters, and the audience. Grove is obviously aware of the boredom factor, and says sternly: "Regard attendance at the meeting for what it is: work."

There is also the mission-oriented meeting, which is "usually *ad hoc* and is designed to produce a specific output, frequently a decision". The problem here is an ineffective chairman who does not know what he wants. Only call a meeting if you know the answer to the first question listed below and can answer "yes" to the other three:

- What am I trying to accomplish?
- Is a meeting necessary?
- Or desirable?
- Or justifiable?

Grove is wary of these ad hoc meetings, which "a manager should never have to call... if all runs smoothly, everything is taken care of in regularly scheduled, process-oriented meetings". This ideal is surely unobtainable, and Grove concedes that 20 per cent of problems and issues must be dealt with in *ad hoc* meetings; but spending more than 25 per cent of your time this way is a "real sign of malorganization".

Three stages of decision

In practice, most organizations make key decisions in *ad hoc* meetings. The critical issue, though, is not the type of meeting, but the process used. Grove preaches (and practises) a three-stage process: genuinely *free discussion* (with no withholding of opinions), followed by a *clear decision* (taking care to achieve clarity of expression), and ending with *full commitment*: "everyone must give the decision reached by the group full support". If the decision proves wrong, you return to the start of the process: free discussion.

This "ideal decision-making model" is easy to follow in theory, but not, Grove finds, in practice. Middle managers "often have trouble expressing their views forcefully, a hard time making unpleasant or difficult decisions, and an even harder time with the idea that they are expected to support a decision with which they don't agree". Yet middle managers are vital in Grove's theory of management, in which rank ("position-power") does not confer "decision-power".

In a business such as Intel, knowledge-power people and position-power people have to make the decisions together: everybody involved in the free discussion stage must "voice opinions and beliefs as *equals* [his italics]". His company's overt signs of egalitarianism, such as informal dress and partitions instead of office walls, have a practical purpose. "Status symbols most certainly do not promote the flow of ideas, facts, and points of view," says Grove. "What appears to be a matter of style really is a matter of necessity."

Peer group syndrome

Another necessity is to overcome an awkward fact: anybody who makes a business decision also possesses "pride, ambition, fear, and insecurity". In this context, the most common problem is "peer group syndrome". At Intel's first-ever management training session, Grove discovered the "peer-plus-one" approach, meaning that equals need the leadership of a more senior manager; otherwise the peers will drift towards "group-think".

If no consensus emerges, "yet the time for a decision has clearly arrived", the senior person must make the decision. A balance must be struck between this necessity and the risk of bringing discussion to a premature halt by intervening too early. Grove repeats that all management activity has an output, "which in this case is the decision itself". The quality of the output is likely to be better, he writes, if expectations of quality and timeliness are made explicit by answering six important questions:

- What decision needs to be made?
- When does it have to be made?
- Who will decide?
- Who will need to be consulted before making the decision?
- Who will ratify or veto the decision?
- Who will need to be informed of the decision?

Grove "can think of no better way to make the decision-making process straightforward than to apply *before the fact* the structure imposed" by these six questions. The six also apply to the planning process. Planning's output is "the decisions made and the actions taken as a result of the process". He draws its structure from factory planning:

"Step 1 is to establish projected need or demand: What will the environment demand from you, your business, or your organization? Step 2 is to establish your present status: What are you producing now? What will you be producing as your projects in the pipeline are completed? Put another way, where will your business be if you do nothing different from what you are now doing? Step 3 is to compare and reconcile steps 1 and 2. Namely, what more (or less) do you need to do to produce what your environment will demand?"

Grove also instructs planners to answer a key question: "What do I have to do *today* to solve – or better avoid – tomorrow's problem?" However, he hardly ever looks at the bound Intel volume called the Annual Plan. Rather, he is interested – passionately so – in how *operating managers* [my italics] carry out their planned tasks, "because the idea that planners can be people apart from those implementing the plan simply does not work". All that matters is their output and "the set of tasks it causes to be implemented".

Ideas into action

- Concentrate on the output of managers, not on their level of activity.

- Move your own activity to the place where your leverage is the greatest.

- Pay close attention to customer complaints and their underlying significance.

- Monitor activities at the stage where least value has already been added.

- Learn to say No as early as possible to work that is beyond your capacity to handle.

- Schedule one-on-one meetings with your subordinates on a regular basis.

- Ask what you must do today to solve or avoid tomorrow's problem.

2

Motivating the team to action

Why companies end up in hybrid forms combining functional organization with decentralization ● Developing and mastering the technique of dual reporting ● **How to control behaviour inside teams** ● Why the role of the team manager is that of the sports coach ● **Using "task relevant maturity" to determine a management style** ● Reviewing performance to develop skills and intensify motivation ● **Why more time should be spent on improving star performers**

Andrew Grove's theories on management are based on the conviction that "the game of management is a team game". A manager's output is not the output of the individual, but that of the unit under the supervision or influence of that individual. Management "is a game in which we have to fashion a team of teams, where the various individual teams exist in some suitable and mutually supportive relationship with each other".

Most management texts concentrate on top management (to which, of course, Grove belongs), but his emphasis goes on teams of middle managers. As he notes, the middlemen and women and their teams are generally parts of larger organizations. He uses the "black box" analogy he applies to productive organizations in general (see p. 40). The black boxes that middle managers oversee are linked to other black boxes, and these linkages of smaller units determine how the organization operates as a whole.

Organizational extremes

Grove describes organizations in two extreme forms. In theory, they can be wholly mission-oriented or totally functional ("function" refers to corporate-wide activities, such as marketing or production). In practice, the two extremes tend to be mixed. But where mission is dominant, the organization is the epitome of decentralization: "each individual business unit pursues what it does – its mission – with little tie-in to other units". This form is rarely found outside conglomerates, which are typically mission-oriented and have the minimum of corporate-level functions.

The entirely functional organization is centralized: the merchandising department looks after merchandising at every location, the human resources people hire, fire, and evaluate employees at every branch, and so on. Grove does not shy away from this centralization. On the contrary, he notes that "legitimate desire to take advantage of the obvious economies of scale and to increase the leverage of the expertise... in each operational area across the entire corporation [pushes] us toward a functional organization."

But decentralization is also strongly justified. "The desire to give the individual branch manager the power to respond to local conditions moves us toward a mission-oriented organization." Since neither alternative is likely to produce acceptable results on its own, the real-world solution is to seek a compromise between the two extremes.

The hybrid compromise

Grove refers to this compromise as the "hybrid organization", of which Intel is an excellent example. The company is organized as a mix of business divisions, which are mission-oriented, and functional groups "that can be viewed as if they were internal subcontractors". The subcontractor analogy is somewhat unconvincing, since about two-thirds of Intel's employees work in these functional units. Grove indeed describes "their enormous importance" and dwells on advantages that go well beyond the evident and valuable economies of scale. For example, "resources can be shifted and reallocated to respond to changes in corporate-wide priorities".

A wholly decentralized company could never hope to manage its resources with equal efficiency. There is also the issue of "leverage" (see pp. 16–17). Grove finds that with a functional organization the "expertise of specialists – know-how managers, such as the research engineers who work in technology development – can be applied across the breadth of the entire corporation, giving their knowledge and work enormous leverage". Summing up, Grove makes Intel's functional groups sound almost benevolent: they "allow the business units to concentrate on mastering their specific trades rather than having to worry about computers, production, technology, and so forth".

The hybrid organization does not, however, have the best of both worlds. A functional group is hit with a flood of demands from the business units, which in turn must negotiate several management layers before they can influence the decisions taken in the functional area. The obvious battleground is the distribution of shared resources, such as production capacity or computer time. "The bottom line here is that both the negotiation and competition waste time and energy, because neither contributes to the output or the general good of the company."

All the same, no company can afford to ignore the benefit of having much of its organization in a mission-oriented form. The argument is simple. Although there is only one advantage, according to Grove, that advantage is decisive: "... the individual units can stay in touch with the needs of their business or product areas, and initiate changes rapidly when those needs change. *That is it.* All other considerations favour the functional type of organization."

Grove's Law

Grove points out that even the conglomerates, mission-oriented as they are, have business units that are likely to be hybrids. His observations lead him to propound Grove's Law: *All large organizations with a common business purpose end up in a hybrid organizational form.* The corollary of that law is that all reasonably large companies must one day cope with the problems inherent in the workings of a hybrid organization. "The most important task... is the optimum and timely allocation of its resources and the efficient resolution of conflicts arising over that allocation." This task falls to middle managers, because, as Grove argues, only they are numerous enough to cover all a company's operations. Moreover, they are very close to the problem of generating and consuming internal resources:

"For middle managers to succeed at this high-leverage task, two things are necessary. First, they must accept the inevitability of the hybrid organizational form if they are to serve its workings. Second, they must develop and master the practice through which a hybrid organization can be managed. This is *dual reporting*."

Dual reporting is something that Intel "stumbled onto... almost by accident... when our company was young and small". It means that an employee has two bosses: one in the line role, say, and another in a functional capacity. Grove knows that what he is describing (and practising) is not ideal: "Hybrid organizations and the accompanying dual reporting principle, like a democracy, are not great in and of themselves. They just happen to be the best way for any business to be organized" − and coordinated.

Make people responsible for coordination, taking them out of their regular daily work, and you create "a subtle variation of dual reporting". This is very similar in effect to what Grove calls "the two plane concept", which is another everyday part of organizational life. "For instance, while people mostly work at an operating task, they also plan. The hierarchy of the corporation's planning bodies lies on a plane separate from the one on which you'll find the operating groups. Moreover, if a person can operate in two planes, he can operate in three."

Multi-plane management

Status may well be turned on its head by the multi-plane concept. Grove cites his own case. When president of Intel, he also belonged to a strategic planning group. In that capacity he came under the group's chairman, who was one of the division controllers, and who, in that role, reported ultimately to Grove. This reversal of the subordinate/ supervisory relationship between planes is not only sensible but beneficial to the boss: "The two- (or multi-) plane organization is very useful. Without it I could only participate if I were in charge of everything I was part of. I don't have that kind of time, and often I'm not the most qualified person around to lead."

One key difference, however, is that the superior-leading-subordinate relationship is relatively permanent, while the subordinate-leading-superior nexus may well be temporary, because the group concerned has a finite life. It may be a task force, formed for a specific purpose, or an informal group set to work on a particular problem. These groups only last as long as the problem, but their use is growing fast. Making transitory teams effective is therefore crucial. Grove advises the same techniques that make hybrid organizations work: dual or multiple reporting and also decision-making by peer groups.

Behaviour inside the teams, and at work in general, says Grove, can be controlled by three invisible and pervasive means: free-market forces, cultural values, and contractual obligations. The (unwritten) contract gives the employer the right to monitor and evaluate and, if necessary, correct work. Both sides agree on other guidelines and work out rules that will be obeyed. When, for whatever reason, the guidelines and rules prove inadequate, you need another mode of control, based on cultural values.

Developing the culture

Management's cultural role is to "develop and nurture the common set of values, objectives, and methods essential for the existence of trust" by *articulation* ("spelling out… values, objectives, and methods") and, more important, by *example*. Fostering the development of a group culture promotes the reduction of "the CUA factor" – the degree of Complexity, Uncertainty, and Ambiguity with which people must contend. The factor rises as their jobs become more involved with "the complex world of multiple bosses and peer decision-making". Resolving the CUA factor, however, is ultimately down to the individual:

"No matter how well a team is put together, no matter how well it is directed, the team will perform only as well as the individuals on it. In other words, everything we've considered so far is useless unless the members of our team will continually try to offer the best they can do."

What if the individual's best is not good enough? Grove sees clearly that there are only two possibilities: the person either cannot or will not do it. To determine which, he applies a simple test: if the person's life depended on doing the work, could he do it? If the answer is "yes", he is not motivated; if the answer is "no", he lacks competence. You have to tackle inability, however caused, by training and/or motivation, the two key weapons for the manager's most important task: to elicit peak performance from subordinates.

As a motivator, Grove relies heavily on behavioural scientist Abraham Maslow's theory that motivation is closely tied to needs, which cause people to have drives, which in turn motivate them. The highest need, according to Maslow, is self-actualization, which stems from personal realization that "what I can be, I must be". Some people are driven to constantly raise their level of competence, others to maximize their achievement. Either way, the drive to perform well has no limit and continues to motivate people to ever higher levels of performance.

Fear of failure

Grove recognizes that fear of failure can be a positive or negative source of motivation. "Given a specific task, fear of failure can spur a person on, but if it becomes a preoccupation, a person driven by a need to achieve will simply become conservative."

In writing about success and failure, Grove often uses sports analogies. He likens the role of the team manager to that of the sports coach. Like an ideal coach, the ideal manager takes no personal credit for the team's success. That earns the players' trust. The coach/manager, though, is tough on the team. Being critical is a strategy for eliciting the best performances. "A good coach," Grove concludes, "was likely a good player himself at one time. And having played the game well, he also understands it well."

One fundamental of the management game, Grove believes, is task-relevant maturity (TRM) – a variable that determines the style to adopt in a particular situation. The TRM referred to is that of subordinates. It is a combination, specific to the task at hand, "of the degree of their achievement, orientation, and readiness to take responsibility, as well as their education, training, and experience".

When the TRM is low, the effective management style is structured and task-oriented; you tell the subordinate "what", "when", and "how". With medium TRM, the appropriate style is oriented to the individual, with emphasis on two-way support and "mutual reasoning".

Football model

Knute Rockne (centre), the tough American who built the Notre Dame college football team into a national icon, stands as a stern model for the "must-win" team manager in business.

Where the TRM is high, the manager's involvement should be minimal, limited to establishing objectives and monitoring. Whatever the level, Grove is adamant on one point: do not deliberately let people learn from their own mistakes. "The responsibility for teaching the subordinate must be assumed by his supervisor, and not paid for by the customers of his organization, internal, or external."

Performance review

A key mechanism in teaching is the performance review, by which Grove sets great store: "giving such reviews is the *single most important form of task-relevant feedback* we as supervisors can provide". Not only is it the means of assessing performance and delivering that assessment, it is also how rewards – promotions, bonuses, stock options, and so on — are allocated. As Grove says, "the review will influence a subordinate's performance — positively or negatively — for a long time, which makes the appraisal one of the manager's highest-leverage activities".

Its fundamental purpose, Grove asserts, is *to improve the subordinate's performance*. Use it to discuss two things: "to determine what skills are missing and to find ways to remedy that lack", and "to intensify the subordinate's motivation in order to get him on a higher performance curve for the same skill level". This is the only time when a manager should act as judge and jury, which makes it doubly important to follow Grove's advice:

"To make an assessment less difficult, a supervisor should clarify... in advance what [is expected] from a subordinate and then attempt to judge whether [the person] performed to expectations. The biggest problem... is that we don't usually define what... we want from our subordinates, and if we don't know what we want, we are surely not going to get it."

Grove draws attention to one big pitfall: the "potential trap". At all times you should "force yourself to assess performance, not potential". Although difficult, improving performance is fundamental:

"No matter how well a subordinate has done his job, we can always find ways to suggest improvement... blessed with 20/20 hindsight, we can compare what

"With the few hours' work that a manager spends preparing and delivering the review, he can affect the work of the recipient enormously."
High Output Management

the subordinate did against what he might have done, and the variance can tell both of us how to do things better in the future."

Level, listen, and leave

According to Grove, three L's should always be kept in mind when delivering a review: Level, Listen, and Leave yourself out. "You must level with your subordinate – the credibility and integrity of the entire system depend on your being totally frank." The instruction "listen" speaks for itself. The third, "leave yourself out", needs explanation:

"It is very important... to understand that the performance review is about and for your subordinate.... At issue are the subordinate's problems, not the supervisor's, and it is the subordinate's day in court."

This sounds as if the subordinate is on trial. If the appraisal is what Grove calls "the blast", that is certainly the case. "You have a subordinate who, unless turned around, could get fired." The initial trouble is that the poor performer "has a strong tendency to ignore his problem". You need facts and examples to cross the first barrier and move the person into active denial that a problem exists. Introduce more evidence, and the subordinate will go further, acknowledging the problem, but blaming others.

Committing to action

The next (and big) step is the assumption of personal responsibility. Once that has been achieved, says Grove, finding the solution to the problem is relatively easy. He feels very strongly that any outcome that commits the poor performer to action is acceptable. The process takes time and trouble, but may prove to be well worthwhile. But what about the excellent performer?

"I think we have our priorities reversed. Shouldn't we spend more time trying to improve the performance of our stars?... these people account for a disproportionately large share of the work in any organization... concentrating on the stars is a high-leverage activity: if they get better, the impact on group output is very great indeed."

Other factors contribute to high output, of course, notably the quality of the interviews that select (or de-select) candidates for employment, and the reward system. Grove applies a simple test on rewards. If the relative pay (what you receive in relation to others) is what matters, and not the absolute amount (the size of a salary or pay increase), you are likely to be motivated in the best possible way – by self-actualization: "because money here is a measure, not a necessity". As Grove summarizes the issue:

"... managers must be responsible and provide our subordinates with honest performance ratings and honest merit-based compensation. If we do, the eventual result will be performance valued for its own sake throughout our organization."

The final responsibility of the manager to the team is training, which Grove considers "one of the highest-leverage activities a manager can perform". He works out that it takes 12 hours of work to give four lectures to your subordinates. If the class numbers ten, they will do some 20,000 hours of work in a year. If the training improves their performance by only one per cent, the company acquires the equivalent of 200 work-hours for the expenditure of just a dozen of yours.

Grove insists that what you teach must be closely tied to practice, and that "training needs to be a continuing process rather than a one-time event". Clearly, for that reason alone, "you and only you can fill the role of the teacher to your subordinates". But there is another reason. "Training must be done by a person who represents a suitable role model... a believable, practising authority on the subject taught."

Training, Grove admits, is hard work: "Much deeper knowledge is required to teach the task than simply to do it." But when done well, "it is nothing short of exhilarating". The output of the team will benefit, but: "Guess who will have learned most... You."

Ideas into action

- Build an organization that is a team of teams and behaves like one.

- Leave the effective allocation of resources to the company's middle managers.

- Be prepared to serve more than one master – even if that means working under a subordinate.

- However high the level of performance, expect it to rise higher still.

- Foster group culture to reduce the "CUA factor" – the degree of Complexity, Uncertainty, and Ambiguity.

- To determine competence, ask, "if this person's life depended on this work, could they do it?"

- To get what you want from subordinates, you must first define your requirement.

Optimizing management

Andy Grove equates his work with that in a production *process. He does not measure his output by hours worked, or any other gauge of personal activity, but by the output of those he manages. Learn to use indicators to monitor progress and ensure that your "leverage" enhances everyone's output.*

Understanding the production process

Grove explains general production principles with his early experience as a waiter, when he was working his way through college. He had to deliver to the table boiled egg, buttered toast, and coffee "simultaneously, each of them fresh and hot". This routine exemplifies the PAT formula of Process, Assembly, and Test.

The PAT Formula		
Process	**Assembly**	**Test**
any activity that physically changes material	components are put together to create a new entity	components or the total are examined and evaluated

In Grove's breakfast task, the Process includes boiling a three-minute egg and making the coffee, the Assembly is setting out the tray, and the Test could be checking on the browning of the toast.

The PAT formula applies to all kinds of productive work, such as training a sales force, developing a "compiler" for a computer, recruiting a graduate – or managing anything. Analyze your own work. How does the PAT formula apply?

Making the production process flow

All production processes have what Grove calls a limiting step – the "longest (or most difficult, or most sensitive, or most expensive) step". You construct your production flow by starting with the limiting step and building around it. In the case of Grove's breakfast, the limiting step is the three-minute egg. Grove works back from the time taken to boil the egg and staggers the other steps to ensure that every stage is completed in good time. Identify your own limiting step and organize the flow of work around that priority.

ANDY GROVE

Focusing on the production essentials

There are five essential parts to every production process. Make these the basis of your approach to your own output, which is judged, remember, by its contribution to the output of others.

The Five Essentials of Production
Build and deliver products...
in response to customer demands...
at a scheduled delivery time...
at an acceptable quality level...
at the lowest possible cost.

Relate the five essentials to your own activities. Ask yourself:
- What are my "products"?
- Who are my customers and what do they want?
- What deadlines must I meet?
- How do I measure quality, and what quality is acceptable?
- What does my "production" cost, and how can that cost be cut?

Your effectiveness as a manager depends on knowing the answers to these questions and using the information to raise performance.

Using your time well

Time is your only finite resource. How well you use it is crucial. How do you divide your time between the three activities seen by Grove as the key functions of a manager?

The Three Activities of a Manager
1 Gathering information and giving it out
2 "Nudging" people to do what is required
3 Making decisions on what has to be done

Write down everything you do in a day under each heading. Are all your activities having a positive impact on the Five Essentials?

2 Managing by measurement

In management, what you measure is what you get. To run any operation really well you need good indicators or measurements, with each one focused on a specific operational goal.

Using indicators for forecasting

Grove envisages the production process as a "black box" that you can look inside. "Leading indicators" provide ways of measuring the process inside the box to see if problems are arising.

- A linearity indicator allows you to draw, for example, a month-by-month straight-line progress from the start of interviewing college graduates to the date when the number of graduates to be hired is supposed to be met. You plot actual progress against the straight line. If there is an adverse gap, act to close it.

- A trend indicator measures output against time (performance this month versus performance over a series of previous months), "and also against some standard or expected level".

A form of trend indicator that Grove has found effective in "getting a feel for future business trends" is the stagger chart. You forecast output over several months ahead and update the forecasts monthly. The chart presents your latest forecast alongside several earlier forecasts. It thus not only tests events against forecasts but also tests the quality of the forecasts themselves.

Optimizing performance

You also need indicators to help determine the most cost-effective way of deploying resources – of getting the most output from the least input. Grove suggests using five critical indicators here.

The Five Critical Indicators
1 The *sales forecast* for the day.
2 The *inventory* of material.
3 The condition of the *equipment.*
4 The *manpower* availability.
5 The *quality* of output.

Take care: indicators tend to make you watch only what they monitor. Concentrating on one indicator at the expense of others can have bad results. For example, focusing on inventory levels might lead to cutting stocks to save money, without anybody realizing that this will create shortages and thus hamper production. Guard against such risks by pairing indicators, so that you simultaneously measure both effect and counter-effect – in this instance, monitoring both inventory levels and the incidence of shortages.

Measuring output

Another mistake is to measure activity rather than output. Do not measure a salesman by his calls, but by his orders and his hit rate. What you measure should be physical and countable. These rules can be applied to administrative functions as well as production, through making the effort to find quantifiable indicators. Grove gives the example of output indicators for office work.

Output Indicators for Office Work		
	Administrative function	**Work output indicator**
1	Accounts payable	Vouchers processed
2	Custodial	Square metres cleaned
3	Customer Service	Sales orders entered
4	Data entry	Transactions processed
5	Employment	People hired (by type of hire)
6	Inventory control	Items managed in inventory

Each of these output or quantity indicators needs to be paired with another indicator that stresses the quality of work: as well as measuring the area of office cleaned, for example, you need to measure the standards of cleanliness.

Draw up a similar list of output indicators for any functions for which you are responsible, and think of a quality indicator with which each of the output indicators might be paired.

3 Applying leverage

The manager's output is that of his subordinates and the unit. You can raise that output by how you use and impart information, get decisions made, and "nudge" people in the right direction.

Gathering the information

Information is the key to Andy Grove's management leverage. He gathers it from standard reports and memos, talking to people inside the company, talking to people outside the company (other managers, financial analysts, the media), and listening to customers.

Grove's most valued way of getting information ("much neglected by most managers") is the walk-about. Make a visit and talk to people as you walk. What takes two minutes on the factory or office floor would take at least half an hour in somebody's office. Do not feel awkward about making visits without any specific agenda. Your objective is to learn – which by definition means that you cannot know what you will discover in advance

Ad hoc communications are Grove's most useful sources of information because they tend to be both quick and timely. Written reports are secondary, but still important, for four reasons:

- They provide an archive of data.
- They help to validate *ad hoc* communications.
- They catch things that you might have missed.
- They force thinking discipline on the writer.

Grove says: "Writing the report is important; reading it often is not." He applies this view even to documents requesting authority to spend capital, when "people go through a lot of soul-searching analysis and juggling, and it is this mental exercise that is valuable".

ANDY GROVE

Learning at First-hand
Intel managers are asked to conduct "Mr Clean" inspections in parts of the company they would not normally visit: the aim is simply to learn.
During the visit the managers check out the housekeeping, the way everything is laid out, the labs (if any), and the safety equipment. The browsing around takes an hour and acquaints them first-hand with processes and people about which they would otherwise know little.

Making the decisions

You need the best information you can obtain to make decisions – or to participate in them, which, says Grove, happens much more of the time. That applies to both kinds of decision: forward-looking (such as capital authorizations), or response to difficulties and crises (either people problems or technical ones). In order to make a correct decision that will result in a firm, clear directive you must know the answers to six important questions.

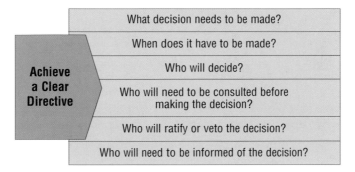

	What decision needs to be made?
Achieve a Clear Directive	When does it have to be made?
	Who will decide?
	Who will need to be consulted before making the decision?
	Who will ratify or veto the decision?
	Who will need to be informed of the decision?

Nudging towards action

Giving information to subordinates and colleagues is equally important – especially in the form that Grove calls "nudging". You may nudge by phone call, note or memo, or making comments in meetings. "You may be advocating a preferred course of action", says Grove, "but you are not issuing an instruction or command." He reckons that "nudges" – pushing people where you want them to go – outnumber unambiguous commands a dozen-to-one.

Nudging is important in meetings as well as in one-to-ones. A meeting is a forum for gathering and giving information and for making participative decisions. Your job as its supervisor is to keep the discussion on track and to have your subordinates or colleagues (preferably all of them) do the work under your leadership. That is another clear example of management leverage.

Always work towards increasing leverage. Keep this key question in mind. Is what I am doing helping others to increase their contribution to the output of this enterprise? If the answer is No, stop doing it, and find something that really will achieve that end.

The loss of Intel's memory

Memory chips are the ubiquitous tools of the computer revolution. In the 1970s, Intel was the prime mover in memories – it had close to a one hundred per cent share of the market – and prospered mightily from them.

A s memory chips grew from 64-bit (meaning that they could store 64 numbers) to 256-bit, then 1,024, Intel remained King of the Memories. But, in the 1980s, a cloud appeared in the East: the Japanese stormed Intel's citadel with ferocious and mounting efficiency.

Reports of Japanese quality results were "beyond what we thought were possible. Our first reaction was denial…. As people often do in this kind of situation, we vigorously attacked the ominous data." This only wasted time, during which the Japanese remorselessly added large and modern factories and slashed prices. Despite this pressure, Intel went on investing in R&D because, "Our priorities were formed by our identity; after all, memories were us."

For a while, the unchanged strategy seemed justified when the enormous impact of IBM's PC, born in 1982, created a surging demand for chips, including Intel's second-string product, the microprocessor.

"Then in the fall of 1984 all of that changed. Business slowed down. It seemed that nobody wanted to buy chips anymore." Orders dried up, stocks soared. Unable to compete with the Japanese producers and their "high-quality, low-priced, mass-produced parts", Intel carried the memory losses on the back of profits elsewhere. Now a new strategy that would stem the losses was urgent.

Intel floundered through "meetings and more meetings, bickering and arguments resulting in nothing but conflicting proposals" and "just went on losing more and more money… We were wandering in the valley of death." In mid-1985, after a year of this aimless meandering, Grove was in his office with his chairman and CEO, Gordon Moore, and asked what proved to be a historic question. "If we got kicked out, and the board brought in a new CEO, what do you think he would do?" Moore answered without hesitation: "He would

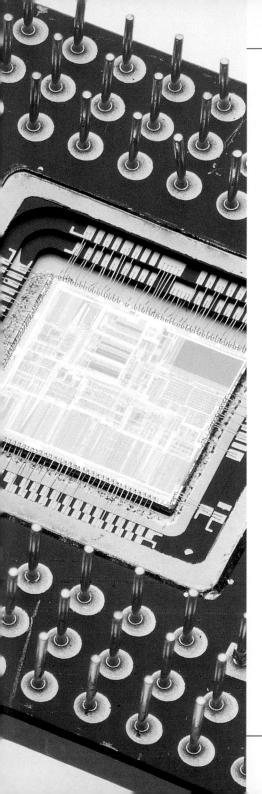

"Had we not changed our business strategy, we would have been relegated to an immensely tough economic existence and, for sure, a relatively insignificant role in our industry." *Only the Paranoid Survive*

get us out of memories." Grove's reaction was to stare at him numbly and say "Why shouldn't you and I walk out the door, come back and do it ourselves?"

This momentous decision – to abandon the very product that had created Intel – has cornered all subsequent attention. Yet what followed was even more important. Grove not only had to force through the decision against confused but serious opposition from senior executives, he had to find an alternative strategy and product. It took a year to implement the exit and throw all Intel's energies into the microprocessor. Fortunately, the 386 was ready for production, and it "became very, very successful, by far our most successful microprocessor to that point".

It took another year before the company became profitable once more. Intel the Memory King was well and truly dead. Intel the microprocessor Emperor was on the high road to $29 billion of sales.

3

Management by confrontation

Using combative paranoia to drive management into a winning game ● How to fit free and freely acting spirits into a regime of tight control ● **"Ranking and rating" employees to exert pressure for improved performance** ● The miraculous birth of the microprocessor which changed the world ● **"Constructive confrontation" as a means of bringing problems into the open – and solving them** ● The debate over the memory business ● **How the psychology of threat leads to market domination**

Practising managers demonstrate their philosophy in deeds, even if, like Andy Grove, they also commit their thoughts and experiences to books. They run a risk when they become authors: what they say and what they do may not be the same; how they behave may be a good deal less rational than how (and what) they write; how their companies work internally may differ from the text.

In Grove's case, inconsistency between words and deeds shows more in behaviour than in the technicalities of management. His day-to-day style, and therefore that of the company, is confrontational. This is clear from the only full account of the man at work: Tim Jackson's *Inside Intel*. Published in 1997, this is a remarkable piece of reporting, written with the active non-cooperation of Grove and the company. Although Jackson's account of Grove's ideas and personality is not meant to be flattering, the book provides essential evidence to support Grove's standing as one of the most brilliant managers of his or any other generation.

Combative paranoia

Even Grove's best-known and highly emotional remark, "only the paranoid survive", has a strong intellectual basis (see pp. 72–85): the company that is not constantly alert to threats automatically becomes vulnerable. The combative paranoia that he describes and uses as a management driver springs not only from his intellect, but also from secretive and aggressive elements in his personality. These explain why Intel went to some lengths to prevent Jackson, a reputable journalist, from gaining access to the sources he required.

Their efforts did not succeed. Jackson discovered strange titbits, such as the stacks of paper next to Intel's photocopiers all preprinted with the legend "Intel Confidential". He found out about the three hours of legal training given twice a year to middle managers, during which they are warned never to say that the company "dominates" the world's microprocessor business, only that it "leads". He also learned about the role-plays in which Intel staff pretend to be law enforcement officers, invade an executive's office, seal it off, and cart away documents to check for incautious words.

Jackson concludes that paranoia works: "this culture helps to explain why the company has become what it is today". The culture reads like one of tight control, which is definitely one aspect of Grove's personality and his management methods. Yet he understands thoroughly that decisions in a highly technological industry must be devolved as far down as possible to people who have great discretion and freedom of action. The formula at Intel is to combine immense delegation with intense control.

The hierarchy that Grove established not long after becoming CEO in 1987 was designed accordingly. He prefers to have only a few people reporting directly to him. So he delegated substantial authority to four senior vice-presidents who headed the key activities: microcomponents, microcomponent operations, systems, and manufacturing. Beneath the quartet, a "management group" enjoyed great delegated powers, but within a framework of tight discipline.

Freedom and control

This results in a series of paradoxes. Managers at Intel are obliged to take the initiative, handling most issues themselves, with minimal upward passing of the buck. When issues affect the whole company, managers create an *ad hoc* group of peers, chaired by a "czar", to solve the problem. But all the free and freely acting spirits must obey the laws of a tough budgeting regime, which embraces all levels. Forecasts of costs and sales are regularly updated, and every deviation from plan must be fully explained.

Everybody in Intel, moreover, has an annual and demanding objective, and this includes the so-called "individual contributors", who have no subordinates and are responsible only for their own results. They, like everyone else, still get an "IMBOS", which stands for Intel Management by Objectives System. MBO is a management control and performance system, long out of fashion, which was introduced to the young Intel by a consultant. It suits Grove's temperament perfectly. MBO slots neatly into a management context whose strong flavour can be judged from this passage in a 1978 Grove memo entitled "Get Organized (Again) – Chapter 2":

"For starters, the Executive Staff decided in reviewing progress against the specific milestones that we set for ourselves that our overall performance in this area rates a 'not done'. Basically, we have not achieved any of the detailed key results that we set in April. Because of that, and because of the continuing immense importance of this issue to both our short and long-term success as a company, we have again decided to adopt 'Getting Organized' as our top corporate objective for the third quarter, with an updated set of specific key results."

You might judge from these words that Intel had done badly. Far from it; shipments of products were much higher, and sales in the second quarter had risen by 17 per cent to a new record. But Grove is relentless in pursuing better results, finding fault, demanding improvements, getting everything down firmly on paper, and expecting excellent performance from all people and all systems.

Ranking and rating

Jackson notes that: "Even before the days of client-server computing, Intel's finance function was so efficient that a detailed set of monthly management accounts was always available three days after the end of each month". The rigour of the financial system is matched by the human resources techniques. Intel has long operated a stiff system of "ranking and rating" employees. It initially had four ratings ("superior", "exceeds expectations", "meets expectations", or "does not meet expectations"). A later version had only three classes: "outstanding", "successful", and "improvement required".

Whether the label is "does not meet" or "improvement required", the implication is ominous. "Improvement required" results in a 60-day or 90-day programme of "corrective action". If this "CA" fails to deliver the specified improvements, dismissal follows. The ranking part of "ranking and rating" is based on the employee's degree of improvement, and is only revealed to individuals in general terms. Their managers, however, see the specific results. These compare employees to each other, and obviously identify those whose services can most easily be lost.

"Ranking and rating" operates with no respect for previous achievements: at Intel you are only as good as your last performance, and you are kept only for as long as you perform well. Dismissal, however, is not the only sanction. Grove will also demote managers who perform badly, moving them to a lowlier job, which at least gives them the chance and incentive to haul themselves back. The whole organization, as well as individuals, can attract Grove's disapproval. In 1981, for example, he ordered the "125 per cent solution": all staff, other than those paid by the hour, were asked to work an additional two hours per day.

Managing the hours

It seems strange that, in a company that can win only by brainpower, Grove should attach such importance to the quantity of hours worked rather than the quality. Ten years earlier, in 1971, the same obsession resulted in the saga of the "late list". Grove was annoyed by late starts to early morning meetings, and security officers were instructed to get signatures from all employees arriving after 8 a.m. The system was widely opposed, much resented, and often evaded (with false signatures, and so on). But Grove insisted on its retention for almost 17 years, finally ending the practice as part of a general liberalization and mellowing.

The whole approach to people and performance, with its emphasis on discipline and enforcement, reflects Grove's own attitudes. Jackson quotes him as saying to one executive that, "fundamentally, you believe that people left to their own volition will do good and not bad. I believe they'll do bad and not good." In Jackson's summary:

> "Grove was not a leader in the sense of someone who inspires the troops from the front, and relies on his own charisma to persuade them to follow. Instead, he was more like a shepherd — signalling with his crook where he wanted the flock to go, but keeping a team of dogs to bite the ankles of any sheep that strayed off…."

The principle of leaving people in charge of their own decisions and projects, but demanding and exacting excellent performance, fits the description "loose-tight controls". The phrase comes from *In Search of Excellence*, the best-seller written by Tom Peters and Robert Waterman and published in 1982. The meaning is obscure in the book — but not at Intel. However tightly everything else is controlled, innovation runs remarkably free. Important advances can be born anywhere in the company.

Microprocessor saga

The results are well illustrated by sagas such as that of the microprocessor, the device that literally transformed the world and saved Intel from extinction. Intel was supposed to be producing several logic chips for the Japanese company Nippon Calculating Machine Corporation, to be used in its Busicom desktop calculator. An engineer, Ted Hoff, proposed a design that would place all the circuitry on one chip. This product could be programmed like a computer, and slotted into any device, not only a calculator.

Hoff was taken away from his "computer-on-a-chip" to tackle other work, but Federico Faggin, a circuit designer, picked up the ball with a colleague. In three months, they produced a working prototype. Top management seems initially to have played no part in the development, nor to have sensed the huge importance of Hoff's brainwave. The Japanese were no wiser.

Later, with the device plainly working, but the calculator market slumping, the Nippon people demanded a price cut. Chairman Bob Noyce joined the action, and his contribution proved to be a masterstroke: the Japanese could have a $60,000 refund if they surrendered their exclusive rights to the chip. The customer insisted only that Intel could not sell to other calculator makers. With that harmless proviso, the mighty microprocessor was Intel's for all time.

The irony was that Intel's marketing people saw no future in this low-priced, low-powered product, with no great market. It took desertion by two employees – to make microprocessors in a start-up company named Zilog – to spur Grove into action. He usually takes a belligerent stance towards people who leave Intel to set up new businesses or join a rival, and he has used Intel's full legal armoury to protect its interests. In Zilog's case, the start-up was simply outgunned.

Shrewd business move

Bob Noyce, chairman of Intel from 1974 until 1979, sealed the company's future when he negotiated exclusive rights to the Intel device which developed into the mighty microprocessor families.

Belligerent style

In Grove's confrontational practice of management, belligerence is shown not only in legal and other corporate responses but in face-to-face ones as well. He has been known to behave aggressively at meetings, insulting and upbraiding an individual in front of his peers. According to Jackson, he can be "abrupt, aggressive, and interrogatory", relishing a fight and seeming "to take a positive delight in shouting at people". The war against under-performance is waged with memos, too. Grove's messages to staff are known as "Grovegrams" or "Andygrams". Woe betide any executive who does not respond swiftly to an Andygram that is marked "AR" – "Action Required".

There is a marked contrast between Grove's often emotional and explosive performance in meetings and the strict, rational controls by which Intel lives. The contrast is within Grove himself. On one hand, he is easily angered: on the other, he is highly cerebral. The same drive that makes his intellect so formidable, though, also results in a passion for detail. Jackson describes Grove as having a fetish for cleanliness and order, and as instituting regular (and unpopular) office inspections. An untidy desk or too many papers in the in-tray means a black mark.

Grove's personality thrives on confrontation. This personal bent has been intellectualized into a system called "constructive confrontation". Although it sounds like a contradiction in terms, it is regarded in Intel as a positive value. It is even taught in formal training, and has a place in the company's statement of values. The idea is to bring problems out into the open, and to debate and resolve the issues pragmatically, without arousing personal animosities.

Agonized discussions

In fact, the defining moments in Intel's history, such as the crisis over the memories business (see pp. 46–7), or the decision not to back the more advanced RISC technology for microprocessors (see pp. 62–3), were marked by long and agonized discussions. On the memory issue, in Grove's own words from *Only the Paranoid Survive*:

"We had meetings and more meetings, bickering, and arguments, resulting in nothing but competing proposals. There were those who proposed what they called a 'go for it' strategy: 'Let's build a gigantic factory dedicated to producing memories and let's take on the Japanese.' Others proposed that we should get really clever and use an avant-garde technology... Others were still clinging to the idea that we could come up with special-purpose memories...."

Even when Grove and Moore, his CEO, produced a fourth alternative, abandoning memories altogether, many opposed this cutting of the Gordian knot. "The company had a couple of beliefs that were as strong as religious dogmas.... One was that memories were our 'technology drivers'.... The other belief was [that] our salesmen needed a full product line to do a good job in front of our customers." The twin beliefs made open-minded, rational discussion "practically impossible".

Note that, although two such strong personalities as Grove and Moore headed the firm, the issues were thrashed out thoroughly, even at the expense of high-priced delays in implementing what, in hindsight, proved to be a brilliantly correct decision. Grove is the opposite of indecisive, but "constructive confrontation" ensures that no alternatives are left unexplored, and that discussion, exhaustive and often exhausting, leads to the right choice, one that is understood − and fully endorsed − by the "management group". The alternative to endorsement is departure.

Confrontation is also a prominent feature of Intel's relationships with competitors. It has a host of mostly friendly alliances, which may include competitor partnerships, but they can turn unfriendly. Advanced Micro Devices (AMD), for example, was a partner in microprocessors, used as a "second source" for the supply of Intel designs. Second-sourcing was a precondition of winning the first, indispensable contract for the IBM PC:

the customer would not proceed otherwise. But the partnership had a most confrontational sequel. Three years of highly charged litigation followed when Intel dumped AMD and went ahead with production of the best-selling 386 chip on its own.

Keeping the market

Some alleged that Grove – not a man to antagonize – was getting his own back for various slights inflicted by Jerry Sanders, the flamboyant boss of the smaller company. But the dumping of AMD had far wider and weightier implications. Keeping competitors out of his markets is fundamental to Grove's strategy. The longer that Intel has a market to itself, the more money it can make from its often huge margins, which are well over 80 per cent on microprocessors. Hence the ferocity with which Grove confronted Motorola in the marketplace, winning with the so-called "Operation Crush" sales campaign in 1978, despite a technically inferior product.

The sheer tenacity of Grove's drive can never be exaggerated. In September 1988, when Intel was deep into its programme for the 486 chip, powerful-seeming rivals, including Sun Microsystems and Hewlett-Packard, were circling around. *Business Week* commented that "Japan is determined to break Intel's grip, as well", and quoted an American rival to the effect that, "This is a break in the action, where everybody gets the chance to play again." Play, yes: win, no. The 486 and its Pentium successor consolidated Intel's power and position, just as Grove had planned. Interviewed in *Business Week*, he said: "My hope and vision is that our technology is going to be the heart, spine, and framework of the entire computer industry."

Given all those circling rivals, Grove's paranoia becomes understandable. He uses it as a tool to make his managers as responsive to change as his engineers. The psychology of threat has been a driving force behind Intel's protection of its "intellectual property"; behind its investments in manufacturing capacity to make its dominant market share all but invulnerable; behind the acceleration in technology that has progressively made microprocessors and personal computers vastly more powerful and vastly cheaper.

Making model profits

In 1988, desktop computers containing the 486 chip were expected to cost $20,000. In 2000, Pentium-powered PCs cost a tenth or less of that amount. Such dramatic falls in prices might look calamitous, but Grove has developed the company's "business model" to a fine pitch of performance. A business model basically hinges on sales volume, realized prices, and gross margins. Intel's model has consistently generated higher and higher profits out of lower and lower prices, offset by higher and higher volumes.

In the decade to 1999, Intel rewarded its investors with a 44 per cent annual growth in total return; only 13 companies in America's biggest 500 did better. Despite massive spending on R&D and capacity, its net margins were the eighth highest among the giants, while its growth in earnings per share hit an astonishing 32.2 per cent per annum – that means doubling every two years, a most extraordinary rate of advance for a $30 billion company. This financial performance provides another key ingredient in Grove's practice of management: enriching staff.

Personal wealth is what makes Intel's confrontational style and hard manners palatable to people who, at any time, can walk out to an excellent job elsewhere. Stock options are very important in the organization's scheme of things. Employees who got in at the bottom when Intel went public in 1971 saw their shares rise from $23.50 to $4,385 in June 1993. The three-year gap between grant and ownership of option shares serves as a golden handcuff – and the higher the shares rise, the tighter the cuffs.

The continuing surge in Intel's shares has created many millionaires and multimillionaires, not least Grove. These rewards have cemented the executive and technical cadres, but crucial to their creation is the confrontational spirit exemplified and inspired by their leader.

Ideas into action

■ Devolve decisions to people who get great discretion and freedom of action.

■ Be relentless in pursuing better results, finding fault, and demanding improvements.

■ Avoid any restriction that makes it harder for innovators to innovate.

■ Operate "loose-tight controls" to combine essential freedom with necessary discipline.

■ Debate and resolve issues pragmatically, without arousing personal animosities.

■ Devote as much time and energy as necessary to thrashing out a consensus.

■ Achieve the optimum combination of prices and volume to maximize profits.

Risking it all on RISC

In the late 1980s, many observers (and several competitors) believed that Intel had finally developed an Achilles heel in its mainline, near-monopoly business of microprocessors. The company itself felt vulnerable.

ANDY GROVE

Intel's huge success had been founded on CISC technology (Complex Instruction Set Computing), which needed many more transistors than the newer RISC (the R stands for Reduced). Now, the 486 chip (right), using the older, slower technology, was deep into its development. Was Intel going to be leapfrogged?

Nobody knew the answer. But Grove was clear on one point. He regarded Intel's microprocessors as a family, with each new chip compatible with the same software as its predecessors. RISC chips were incompatible, so customers would need new software. All the same, with a somewhat heavy heart, Grove threw resources into developing an excellent and successful RISC chip, the i860. He now had two chips, but the company was torn apart by controversy over which one to back.

Development work on the RISC, while initially a necessary precaution, had grown to be "a very large force affecting the company", one that "eventually could have weakened our entire microprocessor thrust. In short, it created chaos."

Since Grove was not himself a computer scientist, he had to rely on his technical experts. But they "had all split into warring camps, each camp 100 per cent convinced of its own chip's supremacy". The customers and partners were also divided: Compaq opted for the 486, and Microsoft the i860.

The turning point came in April 1989 when Grove introduced the 486 in Chicago. Everybody who was anybody in computers was there, and all announced their readiness to introduce 486-based products. "I remember sitting... and thinking, 'RISC or no RISC, how could we possibly not put all our efforts into supporting this momentum?'" Returning from Chicago, Grove ended the fierce debates, and Intel refocused on the 486, and on its equally successful descendants.

Looking back at those debates six years later, Grove was mystified at his indecision: "I shake my head about how I could have even considered walking away from our traditional technology that then had, and still has, phenomenal headroom and momentum." If the decision had gone the other way, Intel's whole marketing platform might have been undermined. The compatibility of its memory chips would no longer have been a massive advantage, and the rival RISC manufacturers would have started on level terms.

"The issue... didn't involve factors that might or might not arise a decade from now; it demanded a decision immediately, and the decision was crucial."
Only the Paranoid Survive

Moreover, wrote Grove in 1996, "the advantages of RISC technology over CISC technology are much smaller than they appeared then". The sacrifice would have been in vain. It was a false alarm, and one of the most expensive in history.

Driving performance

Andy Grove has demonstrated that, to flourish, the best and highest technology needs the best and highest standards of leadership. A manager's most important task is to get peak performance from staff. They need to be selected, motivated, trained, set stretching aims, appraised, and rewarded by leaders who set a powerful personal example.

Modelling the role

Motivation and training – the two key means to the end of peak performance – are both demanding tests of leadership. The more you participate as face-to-face motivator and trainer, the more effective your leadership will be. Every leader is a role model, for better or for worse. You must show the same drive for high achievement that you demand of others.

   Above all, concentrate on creating an environment that values and emphasizes *output*. High motivation and training are useless if they do not advance the output of the unit and the individuals in that unit. Cross-examine yourself regularly with these three questions:

■ Have my actions contributed to higher output?

■ Is my contribution visible to others?

■ Have I shown commitment to higher output still?

Getting your message across

Being a visible role model is easier in a small organization. But even in a small unit, where contacting people face-to-face is easy, you still need to find a way "to project your determination, will, and vision". You can never, says Grove, overclarify or overcommunicate.

Project your Vision	Give a lot of talks to employees.
	Visit them where they work.
	Explain over and over again.
	Answer employees' questions.
	Do not be afraid of repetition.

Working one-to-one

Personal interviews are crucial to leadership. Grove singles out two especially difficult tasks – selecting the right employee and keeping somebody who wants to leave. But one-on-one meetings are essential tools for other purposes, too, and the same three rules always apply.

The Three Rules of One-to-one Meetings
1 Have a clear purpose.
2 Use the interview to learn.
3 Make use of what you have learnt to achieve your aim.

Applying the rules

In a job interview your purpose is to discover all you can: about the candidate's technical knowledge and skills; how well the person used those abilities in the past; any discrepancies, failures, and problems; how well the candidate will fit the organization and its needs. Get the candidate to speak for 80 per cent of the time.

When someone you value says they want to quit, use the three rules to persuade them to stay. Follow Grove's approach:

■ Drop what you are doing and deal with the issue at once. ("Your initial reaction... is absolutely crucial.")

■ Let them talk – do not argue, lecture, or panic.

■ Look for and learn the person's real motives.

■ Buy as much time as you can and need.

■ Seek help and advice as required.

■ Make an offer that the person cannot refuse.

Giving Interviews Top Priority
To maximize the chances of hiring the right people, candidates at Intel may be interviewed by as many as six people, all of whom give interviews top priority.

One interviewer would not stop to take a phone call from the chairman, Robert Noyce, because "I have a candidate". Even Grove gets involved in hiring new graduates. When one star seemed likely to accept an offer from any of a dozen other would-be employers, Grove signed a personal letter telling the young man why he should join Intel – which he did.

1 Management by objectives

Andy Grove ardently practises Management by Objectives (MBO), an idea originally conceived by management guru Peter Drucker. He uses MBO as a control mechanism to raise everyone's performance.

Establishing the system

MBO is about setting yourself objectives and then breaking these down into more specific goals or key results. To get the whole process rolling, you need to answer only two questions:

■ Where do I want to go? (What is the objective?)

■ How will I pace myself to see if I am getting there? (What are my milestones, or key results?)

Make sure that the answers are precise. As Grove says, "The one thing an MBO system should provide is focus." So keep the number of objectives small. Most people disobey this rule; they try to focus on everything, and end up with no focus at all.

Start with a few well-chosen overriding objectives. Next, set your subordinates objectives that fit in with those objectives. Always allow your subordinates to set the key results that will enable them to meet their objectives. At Intel Grove tells his managers to give "the key results very specific wording and dates, so that when deadline time arrives, there is no room for ambiguity".

MBO in Action at Intel
1 Intel manager adopts overriding objective to ensure that all plant expansion projects stay on schedule.
2 He gives subordinate executive particular objective: Obtain decision on Philippine plant expansion by October.
3 Subordinate sets four key results to attain: ■ Study suitable land availability by June. ■ Complete financial analysis of alternatives. ■ Present results to steering group for decision. ■ Get Grove to ratify by October.
4 Grove ratifies, and all objectives are met.

ANDY GROVE

Aiming high

Grove uses MBO to drive exceptional performance by setting exceptionally high targets. He sets objectives at a point so high that even if individuals push themselves hard, they will still only have a 50–50 chance of hitting the target. He maintains that output will tend to be greater when everybody strives for a level of achievement beyond their immediate grasp.

A high-performance system will function best in an organization that consists mostly of people who are not easily deterred and want to maximize their achievement. To determine whether you are an achiever, place yourself in this situation. You are sent into a room where pegs are set around the floor. You are given a set of rings but no instructions. Which of the following would you do?

■ Throw the rings at distant pegs (A).

■ Walk up to the pegs and drop the rings over them (B).

■ Walk back enough to find out your peak throwing skill (C).

If you chose A, you are a gambler, who takes high risks but does not control events. If you chose B, you are a conservative, who takes very little risk. If you answered C, you are an achiever, one of those who must always test and improve themselves.

Taking account of the CUA factor

Grove lays stress on the degree of Complexity, Uncertainty, and Ambiguity, "the CUA factor", in a company, unit, or job. If CUA is high and individuals are motivated by self-interest, chaos will follow. Promote group interest and cultural values to cope with high CUA.

Modes of control

The chart shows how differing types of motivation and levels of CUA require different modes of control. When CUA is high, only group interest and control by cultural values will work.

2 Appraising achievement

Appraisals, or performance reviews, play a crucial role in improving the performance of subordinates. It has two key aspects: actually assessing performance and then delivering the verdict.

Making the assessment

Grove stresses that you should tie an employee's performance to the workings of the organization: "If performance indicators and milestones in a management-by-objectives system are linked to the performance of the individual, they will gauge his degree of success and will enhance his progress."

Use both output measures and internal measures to assess an individual's performance. Output measures "include such things as completing designs, meeting sales quotas, or increasing the yield in a production process." Internal measures survey what is being done to create output now and in the future. The relative significance of output and internal measures will vary from time to time, as will that of short-term and long-term needs.

Carrying out the appraisal

Choosing the right measures will not save you from having to make and deliver personal judgements – which is why most managers so dislike doing appraisals. You are very probably managing the subordinate wrongly if your comments during the review come as a surprise or shock. Follow seven principles of effective appraisal.

Make review comments specific, not general.
Deliver messages consistent with rating or pay increase.
Indicate how to improve.
Appraise Effectively — Criticize fairly but bluntly.
Be fully informed about subordinate's work.
Consider more than recent performance.
Do not deliver too many messages.

ANDY GROVE

Rewarding performance

Andy Grove looks at money and other rewards as a key means of getting high performance. That means dispensing, allocating, and using money to deliver "task-relevant feedback" – the award tells the recipient how well he or she has performed.

Bonuses have to be linked to performance, although not necessarily to that of the individual alone. A bonus scheme might base the payment on three separate factors, each of which would account for a third of the potential total payment.

The Three Bonus Factors
1 How well the individual has performed, as judged by the supervisor.
2 How well the team has done, as measured by objective results.
3 The overall financial performance of the company as a whole.

Grove suggests paying senior managers a bonus of up to half of base salary and middle managers between 10 to 25 per cent.

Reviewing salaries and promotion

Under any system, there is a ceiling for the base salary of every job: what the job is worth. Do not pride yourself on paying below market rates: remember "the labourer is worthy of his hire", especially a good worker. You can set the base salary on the basis of experience only, merit only, or (as most companies do) on a combination of the two. Given Grove's basic principle – using pay to boost performance – merit must come into the reckoning.

Like it or not, any linkage of salary to merit means that you have to accept the need for a competitive, comparative evaluation of individuals. This is also inevitable in another vital means of reward: promotion. Do not consider people for promotion unless their performance exceeds the requirements of the present job: meeting the requirement is not enough. But do not leave an exceeder unpromoted for long. If you do "in time he will atrophy, and his performance will return to a 'meets requirements' level and stay there." That is bad for the employee – and for you.

4

Mastering strategic crisis

How the "strategic inflection point" drives companies into the turbulent waters of critical change ● The six forces that impact on competitive strategy ● **The two signs indicating that "10X" forces are changing an industry dramatically** ● Why the most successful companies are the least likely to accept the need for dynamic change ● **The inexorable trend towards "horizontal" industries** ● Three tests to separate "signal" from "noise" ● **How to achieve broad, intensive, and comprehensive debate**

Andy Grove's great contribution to strategic thought and practice centres round the "strategic inflection point". This technical phrase would have featured in the title of his 1986 book, had Grove had his way, but the publishers thought otherwise. They even rejected it for the subtitle, which now reads "How to Exploit the Crisis Points that Challenge Every Company and Career". But this message is far overshadowed by that of the book's main title: *Only the Paranoid Survive.*

Grove has no recollection of when, where, and why he said this, but it encapsulates his strategic approach to business. He is a world-class worrier. There is management method in what might otherwise seem mild madness. "Business success contains the seeds of its own destruction," he writes. "The more successful you are, the more people want a chunk of your business and then another chunk and then another until there is nothing left." The manager's prime responsibility is to protect the chunks, to defend success.

A world of worries

Grove guards constantly against other people's attacks, and urges subordinates to share this guardian attitude. Fear of attack by no means exhausts the list of Grove's anxieties. He worries about products getting screwed up, or being introduced prematurely; about factories under-performing, or there being too many of them; about hiring the right people and falling morale; about competitors "figuring out how to do what we do better or cheaper" and stealing Intel's customers. "But these worries pale in comparison to how I feel about... a strategic inflection point... a time in the life of a business when its fundamentals are about to change."

While such a point can be caused by technological change, that is by no means all. Competitors may be the cause, but, again, more is involved. "Strategic inflection points are full-scale changes in the way business is conducted." You cannot rely on adopting new technology or battling the competition in the old way. The points "build up force so insidiously that you may have a hard time even putting a finger on what has changed, yet you know that something *has*". You also know that something of this fundamental order *will* happen:

"Technological change is going to reach out and sooner or later change something fundamental in your business world... In technology, whatever *can* be done *will* be done. We can't stop these changes. We can't hide from them. Instead, we must focus on getting ready for them."

For Grove, that does not mean formal planning. You can plan to be ready to respond to any change, but a strategic inflection point is more than just any change. It compares to change in the same way that "deadly and turbulent rapids that even professional rafters approach gingerly" compare to ordinary waters. Grove calls these developments "10X" forces, suggesting that there has been a tenfold increase in one of the six forces that impact on competitive strategy.

1. Power, vigour, and competence of existing competitors
2. Power, vigour, and competence of "complementors" (other firms in the same business system, such as software suppliers vis-à-vis hardware firms)
3. Power, vigour, and competence of customers
4. Power, vigour, and competence of suppliers
5. Possibility that what your business is doing can be done in a different way
6. Power, vigour, and competence of potential competitors

These forces, based on Grove's reading of Harvard professor Michael Porter, tell you how "10X" phenomena may start, but not when or where the inflection point will occur. Technically, this point is where a curve stops curving in one direction and starts curving in another. The "old strategic picture dissolves and gives way to the new, allowing the business to ascend to new heights"; or, if the point is missed, "you go through a peak and after the peak the business declines".

Even in retrospect, it is difficult to tell exactly where a strategic inflection point occurred. So "how can you tell while going through one?" asks Grove. He highlights two signs. First, you are aware of "a troubling sense that something is different. Things don't work the way they used to." You notice changes in customer attitudes, less success in development work, rising competition from disregarded sources, and the "trade shows seem weird". Second, "there is a growing dissonance between what your company thinks it is doing and what is actually happening inside the bowels of the organization".

Division of opinion

The signs, however, will not be read in the same way by everybody concerned. The consequence − another indicator of strategic inflection, presumably − is division of opinion within the company: divergent views about what to do "will be held equally strongly, almost like religious tenets". As co-workers battle and long-term friends fight, management at all levels suffers:

"Everything senior management is supposed to do − define direction, set strategies, encourage teamwork, motivate employees − all these things become harder,

The expert on competitive forces
Grove's "10X" forces – major changes affecting a business, for good or for bad – were based on Harvard professor Michael Porter's investigation of the competitiveness of companies.

almost impossible. Everything middle management is supposed to do – implement policy, deal with customers, train employees – also becomes more difficult."

But at some point the senior manager has "to take appropriate action, to make the changes that will save your company or your career". You do not know that the moment is right, yet you cannot wait until you do know. The only certainty is that the changes are best undertaken while the company is healthy. Act while cash and profits are still being generated and "you can save much more of your company's strength, your employees, and your strategic position".

Beyond that, says Grove, speaking as a believer in scientific management, unscientific instinct and personal judgement are the chief guides through strategic turbulence. History is also useful. Whether it is railroads changing transportation or superstores driving out small retailers, "The lessons and dynamics of what happens seem to be the same, no matter what the industry, no matter where it is located, and no matter which era it operates in."

Grove draws on his own industry, computing, to illustrate the process. Manufacturers, led by IBM, developed along vertical lines, with their own proprietary chips, computers, operating systems, and applications software. The "10X" force was the microprocessor, the core of the personal computer. "Over time this changed the entire structure of the industry and a new horizontal industry emerged" with five different layers: distribution, applications software, operating systems, computers, and chips.

Missing the point

These PC developments are clear, but the exact timing of the strategic inflection point is uncertain, even in hindsight. The critical fact, though, is that all the leading players of the vertical era missed the inflection point – and that included IBM, the only one to launch a successful PC. Its managers were conditioned by the past: "Their long reign of success deeply reinforced and ingrained the thought processes and instincts that led to winning in the vertical industry." They were thus unsuited to the different rules of horizontal competition. Grove draws two lessons:

1. When a strategic inflection point sweeps through an industry, the more successful a player is, the more threatened it is by change and the more reluctant to adapt.
2. The cost of entry to an industry against well-entrenched competitors can be very high, but may become trivially small when the structure breaks.

The break will lead to a new structure that has its own rules. "Horizontal industries, for example, live and die by mass production and mass marketing" – and by their success in a "brutally competitive" environment. Grove lists three rules for brute competing:

1. Do not differentiate without a difference; do not introduce improvements that provide an advantage over the competition but give no advantage to the customer.
2. Act first when a technology break or other fundamental change occurs. The first mover – and only the first mover – has a true opportunity to gain time over its competitors.
3. Price for what the traffic will bear, then "work like the devil on your costs" to make money at that level.

Grove's third rule leads to the economies of scale that make heavy investment effective and productive. The contrasting policy of fixing prices above your costs often leads only to a "niche position, which in a mass-production-based industry is not very lucrative". Although Grove is talking here of horizontal industries, like his own, he is undoubtedly correct in discerning a general trend towards the horizontal. "As an industry becomes more competitive, companies are forced to retreat to their strongholds and specialize in order to become world-class."

Going horizontal

Vertical companies, Grove points out, must be best in class at everything. Horizontal ones have to be the best in only one field, which is self-evidently easier to achieve. Their functional specialization means that they should also be more cost-effective. Other industries will have to learn how to cope as they shift from being vertical to horizontal and encounter the strategic inflection point: "operating by these rules will be necessary for a larger and larger class of companies as time goes by".

Almost certainly, the changes propelling the shift to the horizontal will be "10X" forces, which, for practical purposes, always lead to strategic inflection points. Examples given by Grove include not only the arrival of superstores and the PC, but the coming of sound to the cinema, container ships, and competition in the telecommunications industry. He is impressed both by the variety and the pervasiveness of the challenges. These always produce both winners and losers: "to a large extent, whether a company became a winner or a loser was related to its degree of adaptability".

Intel's adaptability was tested almost to breaking point in the 1984–85 crisis over memory chips (see pp. 46–7). The crucial incident came when Grove and his CEO, Gordon Moore, put themselves in the position of an incoming boss, an outsider completely new to the organization. "We figuratively went out the door, stomped out our cigarettes, and returned to do the job." The task was to exit from the company's founding product of memory chips, and the key to this wonderfully successful decision was "to adopt an outsider's intellectual objectivity".

Such objectivity is essential, says Grove, if "existing managers want to keep their jobs when the basics of the business are undergoing profound change". As he adds, managers who have no emotional stake in a decision can see what must be done (and do it) sooner. Outsiders have only one advantage, but it may be crucial:

"... unlike the person who has devoted his entire life to the company and therefore has a history of deep involvement in the sequence of events that led to the present mess, the new managers come unencumbered by such emotional involvement and therefore are capable of applying an impersonal logic.... "

The memory chip crisis taught Grove this lesson, together with the meaning and impact of a strategic inflection point. He describes how "small and helpless" you feel when confronted by a "10X" force, how confusion and frustration engulf you, how you want to avoid the new reality – but also how you experience "the exhilaration that comes from a set-jawed commitment to a new direction, unsure as that may be". He also learned some basic principles along the way:

- The strategic inflection point is not really a point, but a long, tortuous struggle.
- The points, however painful, "provide an opportunity to break out of a plateau and catapult to a higher level of achievment".
- Indecision magnifies the threat.
- What is happening lower down the organization, without direction from the top, can be crucial.

On the last point, Grove discovered that production resources had been increasingly diverted from memories to microprocessors, "not as a result of any specific strategic direction by senior management, but as a result of daily decisions by middle managers" These unsung heroes had begun to favour profitable microprocessors over money-losing memory chips. "By the time we made the decision to exit the memory business, only one out of eight silicon fabrication plants was producing memories. The exit decision had less drastic consequences as a result."

Bottom-up strategy

Devolved responsibility, in other words, had worked, not only tactically, but strategically. Grove had come across a vital truth. Salespeople know about shifts in customer demand first, before management; financial analysts, likewise, see the impact of fundamental change before anyone else. At Intel, middle managers acted while senior management was still dithering. The moral is clear: involve middle management in strategy and listen to its front-line information at all times.

Such information should help in trying to confirm that a change is really a strategic inflection point. Grove translates this into telling the "signal" from the "noise". In his business some loud noises have, nevertheless, proved to be poor signals. He gives the example of X-ray technology. Backed heavily by IBM but shunned by Intel, the technology proved not to be a "10X" factor in chip manufacture. Nor did another IBM innovation – RISC (Reduced Instruction Set Computing) – take over from Intel's CISC (Complex Instruction Set Computing); this story is told on pages 62–3. Grove suggests asking three questions to separate the signal from the noise:

- Is your key competitor about to change strategy? If people name a key competitor who previously was not one, that may signal a strategic inflection point.
- Is your key "complementor" about to change? If the company that mattered most to the business seems less important, that again may signal fundamental change.
- Do people around you seem to be "losing it"? Keep a lookout out for evidence that very competent people (including yourself) "have suddenly got decoupled from what really matters".

A fourth approach to the problem of identifying fundamental change is to listen to the "Cassandras", usually found among the middle managers mentioned previously. During the Trojan War, the prophetess Cassandra correctly foretold calamity for the Trojans, but nobody in a position of authority believed her. Such disbelief is also dangerously common in modern corporations. Grove points out that, being in the front line, the Cassandras "feel more vulnerable to danger than do senior managers in their more or less bolstered corporate headquarters. Bad news has a much more immediate impact on them personally. Therefore, they take the warning signs more seriously."

It follows that higher managers should take the middle Cassandras more seriously. You do not have to look for them: "they will find you [and] sell their concern to you with a passion". Grove advises you not to argue: "do your best to hear them out, to learn what they know, and to understand why it affects them". He adds that "news from the periphery is an important contribution to... sorting out signal from noise", but he makes a distinction between learning what goes on at the periphery and learning "what goes on in your business".

The latter phrase means getting information from your normal contacts, who will share much the same perspective. For a completely different viewpoint, advises Grove, talk to people who are geographically distant or are several levels below you in the organization. Instinct and experience will show you how to develop "a feel for those whose views are apt to contain gems of information and a sense of who will... clutter you with noise". But the overriding lesson is that, while you must limit the time spent on listening to random inputs, you should be open to them.

Appreciating "10X" forces

Another important lesson is that the first signs of "10X" forces may be distinctly unimpressive. Grove recalls the early days of the Internet, when "getting from one place to another took forever". The Apple Macintosh looked to Grove like a "ridiculous toy", lacking a hard disk, painfully slow, and with a "graphical user interface" whose future seminal importance escaped him. Another big Apple innovation, the hand-held computing device known as the personal digital assistant (PDA), was also a disappointment.

From today's perspective, hand-held computing looks very different; indeed, it is vastly important. As Grove says, first versions of most things usually disappoint: "you can't judge the significance of strategic inflection points by the quality of the first version". His solution is to imagine what this first effort would be like if it improved by "10X". You might still think it uninteresting. "But if your instincts suggest that a '10X' improvement could make this capability exciting or threatening, you may very well be looking at the beginning of a strategic inflection point."

Managing by debate

The key management technique in this situation, writes Grove, is broad, intensive, and comprehensive debate. The more complex the issue, the more levels of management should participate. You need a variety of views, experience, and personality. Bring in outsiders, such as customers and business partners, too. Time and courage are required from all the debaters. Grove advises them as follows:

■ Senior managers: take your time until people begin to repeat themselves and your own gut conviction builds up.

- Middle managers: give your most considered opinion clearly and forcefully, and ensure that you are listened to and understood.
- Specialists: be fully-fledged participants, contributing in hands-on experience what you may lack in perspective and breadth.
- All participants: accept that unanimity is neither the objective nor the likely outcome of the debate, and that the purpose is to enable senior management to come to a more informed and consequently correct decision.

Grove then proceeds to give the warning that fact-based management has real limitations here. He stresses that "data are about the past, and strategic inflection points are about the future". So, "you have to know when to hold your data and when to fold 'em", and when to argue against the data, turning to your experience and judgement, in dealing with emerging trends.

This advice is particularly powerful coming from a man who has little time for those who substitute opinions for fact and emotions for analysis. But Grove never denies the important role that emotions, particularly fear, play in management. "The most important role of managers," he asserts, "is to create an environment in which people are

"Debates are like the process through which a photographer sharpens the contrast when developing a print. The clearer images that result permit management to make a more informed – and more likely correct – call."
Only the Paranoid Survive

passionately dedicated to winning in the marketplace. Fear plays a major role in creating and maintaining such passion." Market victory, he adds, can be powerfully assisted by four different kinds of fear:

- fear of competition
- fear of bankruptcy
- fear of being wrong
- fear of losing

Grove describes fear as the opposite of complacency, as the force that makes him, "at the end of a long day", scan his e-mail for "news of disgruntled customers, potential slippages in the development of a new product, rumours of unhappiness on the part of key employees", and so on. It is why he reads trade press reports on what competitors are doing, and tears out "particularly ominous articles to take to work for follow-up the next day". Fear makes him listen to Cassandras. But the fear he describes is not mere worrying. It expresses the knowledge, reinforced by Intel's own near-tragic experiences in 1984–85 (see pp. 46–7), that nothing fails like success, and that "a good dose of fear" may help to sharpen a company's survival instincts.

Living the culture

This type of fear is the good kind. However, "Fear that might keep you from voicing your real thoughts is poison.... If you are a senior manager... under no circumstances should you ever 'shoot the messenger' [who brings bad news], nor should you allow any manager who works for you to do so." That is a key element in "living the culture". Intel's culture, Grove says, is one in which holders of knowledge power and holders of organization power collaborate, risk-taking is rewarded, and values are incorporated in the management process. "Whatever success we have had in maintaining our culture," he concludes, "has been instrumental in Intel's success in surviving strategic inflection points."

Ideas into action

■ Do not hide from major change: focus on getting ready for it.

■ Embrace change while the existing business is still generating cash and profits.

■ Regard strategic crisis, not just as a threat, but as a powerful opportunity.

■ Confront major issues by adopting an outsider's intellectual objectivity.

■ Involve middle management in strategy and closely observe its practical decisions.

■ Listen to the Cassandras within the organization and take their bad news seriously.

■ Do not rely on past data when deciding on the shape of the future.

The crash of the Pentium processor

On 22 November 1994, Andy Grove was assessing his students' performance at Stanford University, as their part-time teacher, when he received an urgent telephone call from Intel's head of communications.

ANDY GROVE

The message was that CNN was sending a television crew to cover a sensitive story, that of the "floating paint flaw" discovered in Intel's flagship product, the Pentium processor.

It wasn't much of a story, and that was the problem. Grove did not believe that people could become very excited about a division error that one mathematics professor had encountered while working on some abstruse problem. Grove knew all about the design fault. It "caused a rounding error in division once every nine billion divisions". Thus "an average spreadsheet user would run into the problem only once every 27,000 years of spreadsheet use". Intel put rectification in hand, and did nothing more about the problem, which was primarily aired on the Internet.

The trade press picked up on the story, which was described "thoroughly and accurately... And that seemed to be that". The CNN filming, however, changed everything. The coverage was hostile, and the major newspapers joined in. The snowball grew into an avalanche. Users started to call Intel direct for replacement chips, and the company responded by replacing chips whose users appeared to have a real need.

This action seemed to bring the situation under control. But on 12 December, the bombshell exploded: IBM stopped all shipments of Pentium-based computers. As the "most important player in the industry", IBM's move was particularly significant. Heavily back on the defensive, Grove found "all of a sudden" that "instead of predictable success, nothing was predictable... I felt we were under siege – under unrelenting bombardment".

What to do next was decided after a week of struggle. Grove made a U-turn: Intel would replace anybody's part as requested, regardless of "whether they were doing statistical analysis or playing computer games". With millions

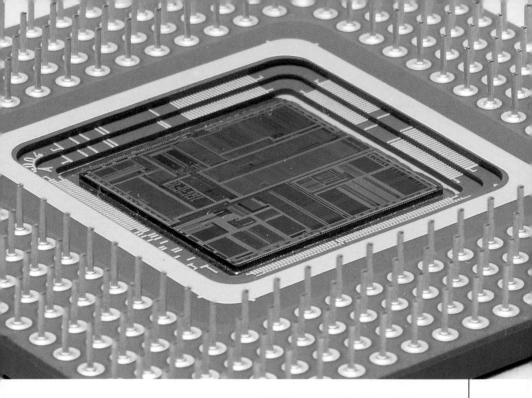

of chips on the market, Intel took "a huge write-off – to the tune of $475 million" as it speeded conversion of chip manufacture and scrapped old material. But, more important, Grove asked a question: "What happened here?"

"Something big, something different, something unexpected," was the answer. First, with its "Intel Inside" advertising policy, the company had identified itself to PC customers as the prime supplier of computing. Second, Intel had become much bigger – a giant – and was now perceived as such. "I was one of the last to understand the implications of the Pentium crisis," confesses

"What was the hardest to take was the outside world's image of us... now the world seemed to treat us like some typical mammoth corporation.... That outside image didn't jibe with my view of us."
Only the Paranoid Survive

Grove. "It took a barrage of relentless criticism to make me realize that something had changed." Intel had to do the same. As a newly fledged consumer powerhouse, it had to behave like a consumer company, not a high-tech temple – so "we embarked on a whole new way of doing business".

5

Coping with change

The four approaches to experimentation and chaos ● How and why managers loathe change, especially when it involves themselves ● **The dangerous results of the "inertia of success"** ● Falling into the dissonance trap of doing one thing and saying another ● **Entering and escaping from "the valley of death"** ● The difference between downsizing and fundamental transformation ● **Why strategic plans fail, but strategic action succeeds** ● The case for deciding and acting sooner rather than later

Although Grove's "strategic inflection points" are among the most momentous examples of change, there are others. He says flatly that "we managers loathe change, especially when it involves us". Like it or not, they are human beings, and "a lot of their emotions are tied up in the identity and well-being of their businesses".

If the change is adverse, their reaction is likely to be emotional. Senior managers who have probably devoted much of their lives to their business feel the pain of sudden, sharp difficulties as a personal loss. They behave as in a real bereavement, but instead of the personal cycle of emotions (denial, anger, bargaining, depression, acceptance), they go through three stages when strategic inflection points occur:

1. Denial ("The Japanese can't possibly achieve these levels of quality.")
2. Escape or diversion ("When companies are facing major changes in their core business, they seem to plunge into... totally unrelated acquisitions and mergers.")
3. Acceptance and pertinent action

Handling change successfully therefore requires replacing denial with brutal realism, concentrating entirely on the front-line priorities, and closing down the gap between awareness and action. Grove actually reproduced a week's calendar for an unnamed CEO confronted by sweeping change. Did the man's allocation of "time, his most precious resource, reflect the strategic crisis?", asked Grove, rhetorically, of course. The answer was an emphatic "no". But Grove may have fallen into the same trap himself:

"Frankly... I have to wonder if it was an accident that
I devoted a significant amount of my time in the years
preceding our memory crisis, years during which the

storm clouds were already very evident, to writing a book... I wonder what storm clouds I might be ducking now. I'll probably know in a few years."

Even if his self-doubt is justified, Grove's writing involved no major commitment of resources. The opposite is true of mergers and acquisitions. These have played a minor role in Intel's rise, which makes it easier for Grove to criticize what happens. The acquisition takes on greater importance than anything else, and the top management will have created "an infinite sink" for its attention.

Even a good leader can be caught in self-created traps, such as Intel's memory crisis (see pp. 46–7). The difference is that the bad leaders stay trapped, while the good ones "eventually emerge to the acceptance and action phases". Often, the inferior bosses are replaced by people who are not emotionally involved in what has gone before. For Grove, this is a key point: "The replacement of corporate heads is far more motivated by the need to bring in someone who has not invested in the past than to get somebody who is a better manager or a better leader in other ways."

Inertia of success

Grove describes the difficulty of the discharged executive as "the inertia of success". Nobody wants to abandon the methods and the strengths that have brought them to a high executive position. "So it's not surprising that they will keep implementing the same strategic and tactical moves that worked for them during the course of their careers...." As Grove says, this is extremely dangerous and can reinforce denial. People almost instinctively cling to the past, he writes, rather than acknowledge that their old skills and strengths are less relevant.

Even if inertia is overcome, "dissonance" can follow. Grove has seen many companies fall into the trap "of saying one thing and doing another". He is clear about what creates this divergence between actions and statements:

- Adapting to change starts with employees who, through their daily work, adjust to the new outside forces.
- Frontline employees and middle managers are therefore implementing and executing actions that say one thing.
- High-level pronouncements continue to say the opposite.

As Grove points out, dissonance is often a clear sign that major change is taking place and that the organization is not responding (see pp. 90–91). Moreover, while "this dissonance between what the company does and what management says is understandable, it accompanies a terribly unproductive and distressing phase". People become confused and uncertain. But light can emerge through the fog. The key process is what Grove calls "experimentation":

- Loosen up the organization: relax controls.
- Allow different techniques, products, sales channels, and customers to be tried.
- Tolerate the new and different.
- Adopt a new maxim: "let chaos reign!".

Here Grove is asking for a great deal. A conservative management will find it next to impossible to go through a phase of "experimentation and chaos". As he says, "you can't suddenly start experimenting when you realize you're in trouble unless you've been experimenting all along". For Intel, accustomed to experimenting in many fields, change is easier and more natural, as the microprocessor saga showed:

"Intel experimented with microprocessors for over 10 years before the opportunity and imperative arose to make them the centrepiece of our corporate strategy... in fact, for a number of years we spent more money on developing and marketing them than they generated in revenue. But we kept at it... and, when our circumstances changed in a big way, we had a more appealing business to focus our resources on."

This sounds tidier than it was. Grove is emphatic that experimentation is not comfortable, especially for a company in trouble. Much better to switch when the existing business is strong. The strengths provide protection, under which "you can make changes far more easily than when the vital signs of your business have all turned south".

The key to avoiding crises like Intel's is to recognize the signs of change and to act promptly. The difficulty is mainly emotional: the "inertia of success" and other preconceptions stop most managers from acting in time. Grove quotes some often heard warning signs:

- "We shouldn't tinker with the golden goose."
- "How could we possibly take our best people away from the business that pays all our salaries and put them on some speculative new project?"
- "The organization can take just so much change; it's not ready for more."

As Grove points out, that last sentence really means, "*I'm not ready to lead the organization into the changes that it needs to face.*" He draws a personal conclusion that no manager dare ignore: "*I have never made a tough change, whether it involved resource shifts or personnel moves, that I haven't wished I had made a year or so earlier.*"

Too little, too late

It is easier to see the need for "tough change" in somebody else's business than in your own. This was the stance that Grove and Gordon Moore took when deciding to exit from the memory business (see pp. 46–7). The problem, however, is not only seeing the need to change, but acting. As Grove observes: "very often we managers know that we need to do something. We even know what we should be doing." The strong manager trusts his or her instincts. Only self-discipline will conquer the "too-little-too-late" syndrome.

If the condition is not forestalled, the company enters what Grove calls "the valley of death". This is the hostile landscape through which the business and its managers must struggle or die. Grove advises that emerging from the valley requires you "to form a mental image of what the company should look like when you get to the other side". The image has to be short and sharp, otherwise it will not communicate to "your tired, demoralized, and confused staff". Grove illustrates the questions that must be answered by using another industry: "What exactly is your bookstore going to be about – will it be a pleasant place to drink coffee and read or a place where you go to buy books at a discount?"

Whatever the answer, it should come "in a single phrase that everybody can remember and, over time, can understand to mean exactly what you intended". The question for Intel in 1986 was whether to be a broad-based semiconductor company, a memory company, or a microprocessor company. The phrase that was "exactly what we were trying to achieve" was "Intel, the microcomputer company". This "mental image" equates with "vision", but Grove typically finds that management buzzword too lofty for the task of capturing "the essence of the company and the focus of its business".

Describing the compamy

Trying to define what the company will be, he stresses, must hinge on defining what it will *not* be. In Intel's case, memories were clearly the main no-go area. But it had significant businesses other than microprocessors. Grove admits that there is a danger of over-simplification, but declares that "it pales in comparison with the danger of catering to the desire of every manager to be included in the simple description of the refocused business... making that description so lofty and so inclusive as to be meaningless".

The short, sharp definition is an act of leadership. Grove recounts his impatience with very senior executives who are torn and indecisive and constantly change their strategic minds; he contemptuously calls this a "direction *du jour*" policy and asks rhetorically: "How can you motivate yourself... to follow a leader when he appears to be going round in circles?" Hesitant leaders are a puzzle to the usually decisive and incisive Grove. He sees, however, that much conviction and courage are needed to move to the front while everybody else is still arguing, and to "set an unhesitating course whose rightness or wrongness will not be known for years".

That is the real test of a leader's mettle. Grove contrasts this type of truly tough decision with the far easier adoption of downsizing. As he says, you need little self-confidence to close factories and fire workers, with short-term financial benefits that will delight Wall Street. Fundamental transformation not only takes longer to pay off, but also involves, as down-sizing does not, escaping from the past that has shaped all parts of the organization. "If you and your staff got your experience managing a computer company, how can you even imagine what a microcomputer company might be like?"

Changing the people

You may well be unable to change the company without changing its people. Grove recalls Gordon Moore, his chairman, saying that "if we're really serious about this [becoming a microprocessor company] half of our executive staff had better become software types in five years' time". Among the converts, of course, was Grove himself, but he, too, needed to learn more about the software world:

> "So I deliberately started to spend a significant amount of time getting acquainted with software people. I set out to visit heads of software companies... met with them and asked them to talk to me about their business — as it were, to teach me."

This learning is easier said than done. Grove had to admit his ignorance and work hard at his self-appointed task. Managers at senior level are "accustomed to the automatic deference which people accord you owing to your position". They find it especially hard to admit that they need to learn new things. Grove was helped because Intel has long been what is now called a "learning company". Learning whole new sets of skills from time to time is part of the culture.

It follows that companies wishing to master change must acquire a similar willingness to learn. This always involves self-discipline, not just in studying, but in allocating time. There were problems at Intel because people accustomed to seeing Grove regularly saw him less often and wondered whether he still cared about their work. This proved a transitional stage, but it makes an important point. Top management cannot expect others and the company to change unless they are prepared to change themselves.

This is a shift of personal resources. Grove stresses that the knowledge, skills, and expertise of your best people are as valuable as material resources. Whenever you shift

Chairman of change
Gordon Moore realized that if Intel were to succeed as a microcomputer company, half of its executive staff would have to change their areas of know-how and become software types.

resources from one task to a new challenge, "you're putting more attention and energy into something, which is wonderful, positive and encouraging". But you are also subtracting production and managerial resources, and your own time, from other activities. Grove's advice is to redeploy all resources to accomplish a transformation; "without them, it turns out to be nothing but an empty cliché".

Strategic action

This commitment of resources to achieve strategic ends is "strategic action". Grove contrasts it with strategic planning, and is convinced that "corporate strategy is formulated by a series of such actions", far more than by the conventional, top-down plans. In his experience, these turn into "sterile statements, rarely gaining traction in the real work of the corporation". The differences are critical:

- Strategic *plans* are statements of intention.
- Strategic *actions* are already taken or being taken.
- Strategic *plans* sound like political speeches.
- Strategic *actions* are concrete steps.
- Strategic *plans* are abstract and usually have no concrete meaning except to management.
- Strategic *actions* immediately affect people's lives.
- Strategic *plans* deal with events far in the future and are thus of little relevance to today.
- Strategic *actions* take place in the present and thus command immediate attention.

The distinction that Grove draws here resembles that between culture and behaviour. Concrete changes in behaviour always change culture, but proposed changes in culture by no means always change behaviour. According to Grove, "the most effective way to transform a company is through a series of incremental changes that are consistent with a clearly articulated end-result." He goes on: "Even if any one strategic action changes the trajectory on which the corporation moves by only a few degrees, if those actions are consistent with the image of what the company should look like... every one of them will reinforce every other."

Grove makes strategic actions sound quite simple, but is quick to point out the difficulties. Good timing is essential in switching resources. They should not be moved from the old task until the full benefit has been obtained. Hang on too long, however, and you may lose a new business opportunity, or lose momentum in a new product area. "Your tendency," warns Grove, "will almost always be to wait too long."

Advancing the pace

Moving too early is likely to be less harmful. Where major strategic change is required, "The risk is that if you are late you may already be in irreversible decline." If you are too early, however, the existing business is probably still healthy and you are thus better placed to alter an erroneous course. Grove strongly recommends that you correct the tendency to delay: "Advance the pace of your actions and increase their magnitude. You'll find that you're more likely to be close to right."

Grove acknowledges that some companies, rapid in response and fast in execution, can operate a "tail-light" strategy, travelling fast in the wake of the pioneers, before catching up and overtaking. The danger then is that, without any rear lights to follow, you may have no sense of direction. Another and increasingly great risk, which Grove does not mention, is that you may never catch up with the early movers. While their main risk is that of being wrong, either in the strategy or its timing, the risk is well worth running:

"The early movers are the only companies that have the potential to affect the structure of the industry and to define how the game is played by others. Only by such a strategy can you hope to compete for the future and shape your destiny to your advantage."

The odds on accomplishing successful change are greatly improved, Grove argues, by adopting a highly focused approach. He quotes Mark Twain: "Put all of your eggs in one basket and WATCH THAT BASKET." Grove argues that all your energies are required to succeed with a single aim, "especially in the face of aggressive competition". The temptation is to try dodging the pursuers by having all sorts of alternative directions – by "hedging". Grove will not hedge, because it is expensive and dilutes commitment.

Clarity of direction

Meandering, moreover, has intolerable side-effects. Managers are demoralized, and when that happens, nothing works, and every employee feels paralyzed. "This is exactly when you need to have a strong leader setting a direction. And it doesn't have to be the best direction – just a strong, clear one." Organizations in crisis, says Grove, are "very sensitive to obscure or ambiguous signals from their management". Conflicting messages also breed confusion. In an uncertain environment, facing an uncertain future, people need to know clearly where they are heading.

The need for clarity of direction, says Grove, increases as the change process develops. No longer do you need to let chaos reign as the alternatives are explored. "To lead your organization out of the resulting ambiguity and to energize your staff toward a new direction, you must rein in chaos." That requires five steps:

- Stop experimenting.
- Issue totally clear "marching orders".
- Commit the organization's resources.
- Commit your personal resources.
- Be a role-model for change.

The ideal is to have an organization that can deal with the two phases: debate (where chaos reigns) and a determined march forward (where chaos is reined in). This, says Grove, is a powerful, adaptive organization with two key attributes:

- It tolerates and even encourages vigorous debates, devoted to exploring issues, indifferent to rank, and including individuals of varied backgrounds.

■ It can make and accept clear decisions, which then receive unanimous support.

This is neither a "bottom-up" nor a "top-down" company. Grove identifies "bottom-up" with empowering middle managers, which seems unduly dismissive of other staff. However, the initiatives taken from below must meet half-way the actions generated by senior management. "The best results," says Grove, "seem to prevail when 'bottom-up' and 'top-down' are equally strong." Combine this dialectic with that between reigning chaos and chaos reined-in, and change need bring no fears to any company.

Ideas into action

■ If you get caught in a self-created trap, acknowledge it – and strive to escape.

■ Start experiments with new methods or new business ideas as often as possible.

■ Make tough changes, involving people or resources, earlier rather than later.

■ Define what the company means in a short, incisive, and convincing statement.

■ Set a firm and decisive course, even if the results will take time to appear.

■ Once you have decided to act, make all necessary resources fully available.

■ Concentrate your energies on a single aim, especially when facing aggressive competition.

Mastering change

*A*nticipating and exploiting change is the key to success in *the 21st century. You need to recognize the signs of change early and then develop a timely strategy to cope with it. You must also make sure that you carry people with you in the transformation of the organization.*

Profiting from paranoia

Whether or not you agree with Andy Grove's maxim "only the paranoid survive", the thought is a powerful tool for effective management of change. Strictly speaking, paranoia is a delusion: but the existence of competitive and other threats, whatever your industry, is likely to be only too real.

Take your guide from what is happening in the present and forget what has happened in the past in your business, which may be wholly irrelevant. Fight against the tendency to stick to the business and the methods that have sustained your fortunes for so long.

Avoiding denial

The opposite of healthy paranoia is unhealthy denial. Change that comes in the form of bad news tends to be denied. To avoid denial, analyze your response to such change honestly and rationally.

Dealing with Bad News
Do I want this news to be wrong?
Is that why I am denying it?
Have I conducted a thorough, dispassionate analysis that shows it to be wrong?
What will be the worst possible result if the news is right and I have done nothing?
What action can and should I take if the news is right?
What is the worst possible result of that action?
What is the best possible result of that action?

ANDY GROVE

Rational evaluation of a possibly threatening change as soon as it appears undermines false optimism and demonstrate what risks you are running through denial and inaction. Remember Andy Grove's words: "Looking back over my own career, I have never made a tough change, whether it involved resource shifts or personnel moves, that I haven't wished I had made a year or so earlier."

Look back over your career. Were there any events of which you would say the same as Grove? Ask yourself why you delayed. Almost always, the answer lies in your emotions; for example, fear of confrontation or fear of being wrong.

Shifting resources

The critical moment comes when you must commit resources to a new product or process. There are dangers in moving too early or too late, although acting too late incurs the greater penalties.

Resource Shift Dilemma		
Resource shift is premature	**Timing of shift is right**	**Resource shift is late**
Existing strategy not satisfactorily completed.	Momentum of existing strategy is still positive; new line builds steadily.	Opportunity for transformation is lost; decline may be irreversible.

The penalty of lateness is very possibly fateful. Proceed on the paranoid assumption that you will never catch up, which will almost certainly be true. Conversely, you probably can turn back and repair at least some of the damage done by shifting resources too early.

Playing Catch-up

The dangers of shifting resources too late are highlighted by IBM's late entry into the lap-top market, in which it has yet to catch up with its main rivals.

IBM launched its mini-computer 14 years after Digital Equipment, and its PC four years after the launch of the Apple II. In both cases the IBM products were successful. But when

IBM came five years late into the lap-top market, Toshiba was the strong leader in a market already worth $6 billion a year. IBM thought it would again catch up. It never has done.

1 Managing the change

Every organization, sooner or later, comes up against the "strategic inflection point" when past success levels off. Develop a new strategy before your existing products and markets begin to falter.

Exploiting the strategic inflection point

Do not regard the strategic inflection point as a threat. On the contrary, it is a great opportunity. When Intel at last responded to the crushing Japanese competition in memory chips, it soared to remarkable new heights by exploiting its microprocessors. The delay in leaving the memory chip market was overcome because the new business had been developed while the old one was still strong.

Intel's management of this particular strategic inflection point contains two essential lessons.

■ Keep your existing business in the best possible condition. Your business is only as good as its latest results.

■ Take all adverse trends in actual and forecast results as calls to action; that is, continually develop new products, new markets, new technologies, new processes, and new people.

Business goes on to new heights

Inflection point

Business declines

Inflection curve
To ensure business success in the face of an inflection point develop your new strategy while maintaining the old.

Developing the new

Use the "windows of opportunity" method to identify which new products and markets could be usefully developed or expanded.

■ Draw a matrix with existing products on the left-hand side.

■ Put your existing customers along the bottom.

■ Extend the left-hand side upwards with dotted lines for products under development.

■ Extend the bottom line to the right with dotted lines for potential new customers.

ANDY GROVE

- Tick each square where you have a customer for an existing product.
- The empty squares are your "windows of opportunity".

Identifying the competition

You cannot develop a successful strategy in a vacuum. Who are your competitors? What are they doing or are likely to do? It is all too easy to concentrate on the rivals you have always faced, even though this may no longer be appropriate. Everybody in computers kept focused on IBM, for example, and ignored the rise of smaller PC makers who were, in fact, dramatically changing the industry. To avoid such dangers, Grove advises using the "silver bullet" test.

The Silver Bullet Test
Imagine that you and your colleagues have one gun and just one silver bullet each.
Ask everybody, including yourself, which competitor they would choose to shoot down by the silver bullet.
Expect a quick, unequivocal answer but follow up by asking, "Are you 100 per cent sure?"
If either the first or second answers betray uncertainty, or come up with unexpected names, sit up and take notice.

Facing the future

"When the importance of your competitors shifts," says Grove, "it is often a sign that something significant is going on." Do not brush new competition aside, or concentrate on its weaknesses.

Making the Future Happen
With the microprocessor, Intel proved the validity of the words of the great PC pioneer, Alan Kay, who said: "The best way to predict the future is to invent it."

The untried, unfamiliar micro-processors started with only a few customers, an apparently tiny market and no profits; "in fact, for a number of years we spent more money on developing and marketing them than they generated in revenue". But when circumstances changed "in a big way", Intel had a new and far brighter future to pursue – and to make happen.

2 Turning the organization

Change cannot be managed without changing people, which means producing different and appropriate behaviour. Achieve this by involving everybody in clear and clearly executed change strategies.

From planning to action

A plan is only as good as the actions that it generates. Many managers spend too much thought on planning and too little on the vital matter of implementation. Andy Grove tells you to test any plan with the following questions:

- Is it just a statement of intention?
- Does it sound like a political speech?
- Does it have concrete meaning only to management?
- Does it deal with events far in the future?
- Does it have little relevance to today?

If you answer Yes to any of these questions, the plan is likely to be as ineffective as most strategic planning. It will not achieve the object of change management, which is to alter people's behaviour – what they do. Grove therefore gives much higher value to strategic actions. To earn his praise, your plan should contain actions.

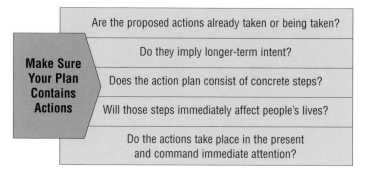

Make Sure Your Plan Contains Actions

Are the proposed actions already taken or being taken?

Do they imply longer-term intent?

Does the action plan consist of concrete steps?

Will those steps immediately affect people's lives?

Do the actions take place in the present and command immediate attention?

Communicating effectively

Make sure that everybody hears about your plan: the proposals, the intent, the concrete steps, what it will mean for them, and what is expected of them. However much you communicate, remember, it is never enough. And listen to your staff, often and hard. People all the way down the company are quite capable of seeing what needs to be

ANDY GROVE

done, and what needs to be done differently. They are simply unused to being heard, let alone to having their recommendations followed. They are an invaluable source of information and action.

As Grove says: "The process of adapting to change starts with employees who, through their daily work, adjust to the new outside forces." Hold a lot of discussions with employees in their workplaces. Ask questions of these experts. Repeat their answers back to them to be sure you have understood. Act on the valuable lessons you learn, and let them know that you have acted.

Achieving a synthesis

You want neither top-down management nor bottom-up, but a synthesis of the two. The chart shows what Grove calls a "dynamic dialectic". The best place by far is the top right-hand square, where both the actions coming down and the actions coming up are strong.

	Bottom-up action weak → strong	
Top-down action strong	Sometimes copes with change	Copes well with change
weak	Fails to cope with change	Fails to cope with change

Dynamic dialectic
This matrix shows that organizations cope best with change when top-down and bottom-up actions are equally strong, balancing management direction with staff participation.

You can have a largely bottom-up system for strategic planning (Intel once did) but that will not cope with "big-time change". Managing such a change requires three elements:
- Vigorous debates in which everyone participates in discussing and arguing about the issues.
- Clear and timely decision-making.
- Total support for the decision once taken.

Merely adopting these elements, for most organizations, will represent enormous change. Trying to manage major change without them is unlikely to succeed.

GLOSSARY

"BLACK BOX": Grove's metaphor for all the processes in any business operation that converts inputs into final output.

CISC: Complex Instruction Set Computing; technology used for Intel's past and present family of microprocessors (see also RISC).

CONFRONTATION, CONSTRUCTIVE: Thrashing out issues by direct, vigorous debate, without personal attacks.

CUA FACTOR: The amount of Complexity, Uncertainty, and Ambiguity with which people most contend in their jobs.

DUAL REPORTING: Being responsible to two superiors – for example, a line manager and a functional director.

HORIZONTAL: Refers to a company or industry organized around specific competences. This has become the prevailing mode (see also VERTICAL).

HYBRID: Organization that is built neither wholly around corporate-wide functions nor on total decentralization.

IMBOS: Intel Management by Objectives System; method of achieving collective performance by setting individual aims.

LEVERAGE: Achieving higher output than possible by the manager's direct contribution – for example, by delegation and motivation.

MEETINGS, PROCESS-ORIENTED: regular meetings (departmental or interdepartmental) for exchange and sharing of knowledge.

MEETINGS, MISSION-ORIENTED: *ad hoc* meetings called to achieve a specific purpose, such as taking a decision.

MEMORY CHIPS: The foundation of Intel's original fortunes; key building blocks of the electronic revolution.

MICROPROCESSOR: "Computer on a chip"; the integrated circuit at the heart of all PCs, and nearly all other modern computers.

MOORE'S LAW: Famously predicts that integrated circuits will double in power and speed at a constant cost every 18 months.

MULTI-PLANE CONCEPT: Having the same person work on two or more planes – for example, in both an operating and a planning role.

ONE-TO-ONE: Meeting between a manager and his subordinate, impromputu or (very important at Intel) regularly scheduled.

PARANOIA, HEALTHY: Grove's term for fear of adverse events, especially competition, that inspires effective action.

PEER GROUP SYNDROME: Tendency of meetings to degenerate into "group-think" in the absence of a senior discussion leader.

PENTIUM: Latest generations of Intel microprocessor family, which goes back to the 8088 chip for IBM's PC, born in 1982.

RANKING AND RATING: Intel system for assessing employees, "rating" their performance and "ranking" them against others.

RISC: Reduced Instruction Set Computing; rival, later chip technology. Advantages over CISC (q.v.) proved insufficient.

STRATEGIC INFLECTION POINT: Where 10X forces (q.v.) begin to impact an industry in what will become dramatic change.

TASK-RELEVANT MATURITY (TRM): Degree to which employees are equipped to take responsibility for the task.

10X FORCE: A very great increase (say, tenfold) in one of the key forces that impact on competitive strategy.

VERTICAL: Organizing a company around all the activities required in an industry. Overtaken by horizontal principle (q.v.).

BIBLIOGRAPHY

Andy Grove's two prime books on managing are unique pieces of work. Both *High Output Management* (first published in 1983) and *Only the Paranoid Survive* (published 13 years later) are genuine guides for practising managers – and not the more typical tycoon memoirs, often self-serving and generally ghost-written. These two challenging and stimulating books bear the highly individual stamp of a top manager with the rare ability to intellectualize his activities. The books naturally draw on Grove's experiences at Intel, and contain much fascinating corporate material: but the latter is used strictly for illustrative purposes.

Grove's first book is far less well known, at least to the general public. Very many students, however, have used this 1967 textbook, *Physics and Technology of Semiconductor Devices*. It is a product of his early academic career, just as *Only the Paranoid Survive* reflects Grove's later part-time academic work teaching strategy at Stanford University. *High Output Management* is a highly practical guide to all aspects of running an effective business. His fourth book, *One-on-One with Andy Grove*, is now out of print. It was an entry in the crowded self-management field, and is subtitled "How to Manage Your Boss, Yourself, and Your Co-workers".

Intel, Grove's part-creation, has received surprisingly little literary attention considering its extreme importance in the digital revolution. *Creating the Digital Future* is a 1998 study, by insider Albert Yu, of how that great contribution has been and is being made. *Inside Intel* is by an outsider, the journalist and later e-entrepreneur Tim Jackson, who braved Grove's and Intel's opposition to produce an unauthorized but authoritative account of a fascinating corporate history. Grove is inevitably its hero – and sometimes its anti-hero.

Works cited

Andrew S. Grove (1983) *High Output Management*, Random House, New York
– (1996) *Only the Paranoid Survive*, HarperCollins, New York
Tim Jackson (1997) *Inside Intel*, HarperCollins, New York

Index

ANDY GROVE

INDEX

Robert Heller

Robert Heller is himself a prolific author of management books. The first, *The Naked Manager*, published in 1972, established Heller as an iconoclastic, wide-ranging guide to managerial excellence – and incompetence. Heller has drawn on the extensive knowledge of managers and management acquired as the founding editor of *Management Today*, Britain's premier business magazine, which he headed for 25 years. Books such as *The Supermanagers* and *In Search of European Excellence* address the ways in which the latest ideas on change, quality, and motivation are providing new routes to business success. In 1990 Heller wrote *Culture Shock*, one of the first books to describe how IT would revolutionize management. Since then, as writer, lecturer, and consultant, Heller has continued to tell managers how to "Ride the Revolution", the title of his 2000 book, written with Paul Spenley. His books for Dorling Kindersley's Essential Managers series are international bestsellers.